Spike Lee

DIRECTOR

Black Americans of Achievement

LEGACY EDITION

Muhammad Ali

Maya Angelou

Josephine Baker

George Washington Carver

Ray Charles

Johnnie Cochran

Frederick Douglass

W.E.B. Du Bois

Jamie Foxx

Marcus Garvey

Savion Glover

Alex Haley

Jimi Hendrix

Gregory Hines

Langston Hughes

Jesse Jackson

Scott Joplin

Coretta Scott King

Martin Luther King, Jr.

Spike Lee

Malcolm X

Bob Marley

Thurgood Marshall

Barack Obama

Jesse Owens

Rosa Parks

Colin Powell

Condoleezza Rice

Chris Rock

Clarence Thomas

Sojourner Truth

Harriet Tubman

Nat Turner

Madam C.J. Walker

Booker T. Washington

Oprah Winfrey

Tiger Woods

Black Americans of Achievement

LEGACY EDITION

Spike Lee

DIRECTOR

Dennis Abrams

CHELSEA HOUSE
PUBLISHERS
An imprint of Infobase Publishing

Spike Lee

Chelsea House
An imprint of Infobase Publishing
132 West 31st Street
New York NY 10001

Library of Congress Cataloging-in-Publication Data

Abrams, Dennis, 1960-
  Spike Lee / Dennis Abrams. — Legacy ed.
     p. cm. — (Black Americans of achievement)
  Includes bibliographical references and index.
  ISBN 978-1-60413-043-0 (hardcover)
  1. Lee, Spike. 2. Motion picture producers and directors—United States--Biography. 3. African American motion picture producers and directors—Biography. I. Title. II. Series.

  PN1998.3.L44A62 2008
  791.430233092—dc22
  [B]
                          2008010496

Chelsea House books are available at special discounts when purchased in bulk quantities for businesses, associations, institutions, or sales promotions. Please call our Special Sales Department in New York at (212) 967-8800 or (800) 322-8755.

You can find Chelsea House on the World Wide Web at
http://www.chelseahouse.com

Series design by Keith Trego
Cover design by Keith Trego and Jooyoung An

Printed in the United States of America

Bang ML 10 9 8 7 6 5 4 3 2 1

This book is printed on acid-free paper.

All links and web addresses were checked and verified to be correct at the time of publication. Because of the dynamic nature of the web, some addresses and links may have changed since publication and may no longer be valid.

Contents

1 The Storm 1

2 "A Very Tough Baby" 8

3 Spike's Gotta Make It 22

4 Color Craze 37

5 Do the Race Thing 45

6 When a Man Loves Two Women 55

7 Ebony and Ivory 65

8 The Ultimate Test 74

9 Spike Chills Out 88

10 Back on Top 111

Selected Filmography 118

Chronology 120

Further Reading 122

Index 124

About the Author 129

The Storm

Sometime on August 23, 2005, Tropical Depression Twelve
formed over the southeastern Bahamas, caused by the interac-
tion of a tropical wave and the remains of Tropical Depression
Ten (a tropical depression is a group of thunderstorms). The
next morning, August 24, the system was upgraded to tropical
storm status and given the name *Katrina*. The tropical storm
continued to move toward Florida, becoming a hurricane
only two hours before making landfall between Hallandale
Beach and Aventura, Florida, on the morning of August 25.
As expected, the storm weakened over land, but it quickly
regained hurricane status after entering the Gulf of Mexico.

Moving over the warm waters of the gulf, the storm quickly
intensified, reaching Category 3 intensity on the Saffir-Simp-
son Hurricane Scale and becoming the third major hurricane
of the season. By August 26, computer models had increas-
ingly shifted the path of Katrina toward a direct hit on the

city of New Orleans. This possibility was considered a potential disaster because parts of the city are below sea level. For this reason, emergency management officials in New Orleans feared that the storm surge in the gulf caused by Katrina could go over the tops of the levees (walls) built to protect the city and cause major flooding. (A storm surge is simply water pushed toward the shore by the force of the winds swirling around the storm. This surge, combined with normal tidal action, can increase the mean water level 15 feet or more, a level that is often deadly.)

Shortly before Katrina was upgraded to a Category 5 storm (the highest category, with sustained winds of more than 155 miles per hour), New Orleans mayor Ray Nagin ordered the first-ever mandatory evacuation of the city. Nearly 80 percent of the area's population fled, but with money for fuel and cars in short supply and all public transportation shut down in advance of the storm's arrival, tens of thousands of New Orleanians, predominantly poor African Americans plus many sick and elderly people, found themselves trapped in the city, waiting for Katrina.

On August 29, Katrina, now downgraded to Category 3, made landfall near Buras, Louisiana. Although the winds that New Orleans experienced were likely only Category 1 or Category 2, the storm surge led to 53 levee breaches in the federally-built levee system that protects metropolitan New Orleans. The Mississippi River Gulf Outlet (MRGO) breached its levees in approximately 20 places, flooding much of east New Orleans, most of St. Bernard Parish, and the east bank of Plaquemines Parish. The major levee breaches in the city included those at the 17th Street Canal levee, the London Avenue Canal, and the wide, navigable Industrial Canal, leaving approximately 80 percent of the city flooded.

Most of the major roads that lead in and out of the city were damaged or closed. There was no power and no drinking water. Some residents of the city, desperately searching for

Many of the communities located along the Gulf Coast lie less than 10 feet above sea level. When Hurricane Katrina hit the Gulf Coast, the storm surges raised water levels so high that they completely surpassed the usual high tide level, as shown in the graphic above.

food and water, began to loot stores. (Others stole nonessential items as well.) Isolated by water from the outside world, the city was in dire straits, and neither the state government nor the federal government seemed able or willing to step in to assist New Orleans and its suffering citizens.

It is unlikely that anyone who saw the images on television of New Orleans during those horrible days after the storm will ever forget them. People stranded on rooftops pleading to be rescued, refugees trapped in the Superdome without adequate food or water, dead bodies floating down the streets of the devastated city—these are among the images that were seared into the collective consciousness of the people of the world. Among those staring at their televisions in disbelief was one of America's leading filmmakers, African-American director Spike Lee. As the days unfolded and no assistance came to those in need, Lee knew that he would have to make a film to show the world exactly what happened to New Orleans and who allowed it to happen.

In an interview with HBO, Lee explained why he felt the need to direct a documentary about the storm, a movie that would be titled *When the Levees Broke: A Requiem in Four Acts*. Lee said,

When Hurricane Katrina went through New Orleans or around it, I was in Venice, Italy, at a film festival. It was a very painful experience to see my fellow American citizens, the majority of them African-Americans, in the dire situation they were in. And I was outraged with the slow response of the federal government. And every time I'm in Europe, any time something happens in the world involving African-Americans, journalists jump on me, like I'm the spokesperson for 45 million African-Americans, which I'm not. But many of them expressed their outrage too. And one interesting thing is that these European journalists were saying the images they were seeing looked like they were from a third world country, not the almighty United States of America.

It was around that time that I decided that I would like to do this. And as soon as I got back to New York, I called up (HBO's) Sheila Nevins, and we met, and she agreed to go forward. What many people say in this film is what happened in New Orleans is unprecedented. Never before in the history of the United States has the federal government turned its back on its own citizens in the manner that they did, with the slow response to people who needed help.

The question then is this: How exactly did Spike Lee become the spokesman, the "go-to" guy when the media wanted a comment on anything African American? The answer is clear: In a film career that spans more than 20 years, Lee has established himself as one of America's premier filmmakers, a director whose films explored the many aspects of the African-American experience. In addition, because of his work as an actor in both his own films and in a series of hugely popular advertisements for Nike with Michael Jordan, as well as his numerous appearances on television, Spike Lee is perhaps the most instantly identifiable living director—of any race.

Spike Lee answers questions during a press conference at the New Orleans Arena in August 2006. Lee was there to comment on his documentary about the aftermath of Hurricane Katrina, called *When the Levees Broke: A Requiem in Four Acts.* With him is historian Douglas Brinkley, who appeared in the film.

Never one to shy away from controversy, Lee, the man who, in his own words, single-handedly "broke the color barrier" in Hollywood in the mid 1980s, uses film to raise questions and provoke discussion. His abrasive, often in-your-face manner had been the basis of his previous films, making them more than just entertainment.

Whether tackling sexual roles in his breakthrough first film, *She's Gotta Have It,* class conflict and racial prejudice among blacks in *School Daze,* sexual mythology in *Jungle Fever,* jazz in *Mo' Better Blues,* racism and police brutality in *Do the Right*

Thing, and African-American family life in *Crooklyn*; giving a satirical spin to the roles of African Americans in *Bamboozled*; dissecting a city under siege by a serial killer in *Summer of Sam*; reminding Americans about the costs of the struggle for civil rights in *4 Little Girls*; or telling the story of an African-American leader in *Malcolm X*, Lee has always attempted to enlighten and educate his audience while at the same time creating characters and presenting a vision of African-American life never before seen on screen. In doing so, he became America's best-known, and most widely respected, African-American film director.

Such fame did not come without cost. Lee is perhaps as well-known for stirring up controversy as he is for his films. He has been accused of being racist, anti-Semitic, and sexist. He has garnered headlines for his comments on former Mississippi Senator Trent Lott, whom he called a "card-carrying member of the Ku Klux Klan" on ABC's *Good Morning America*, and for suggesting that the United States government intentionally ignored the plight of black Americans affected by Hurricane Katrina.

Indeed, it is hard to find anyone who does not have an opinion regarding Spike Lee. Legendary actor, writer, and director Ossie Davis called him "one of the solid rocks upon which current African American culture is founded," and Keir Graff said that Lee is "one of our least predictable, most important

DID YOU KNOW?

Did you know that Spike Lee is the author of two children's books? With his wife, Tonya Lewis Lee, he wrote *Please, Baby, Please*, and *Please, Puppy, Please*. *Please, Baby, Please* is based on a famous line from Lee's film *She's Gotta Have It*. The idea of writing a book for children, as well as the title, though, came from Lee's wife.

film makers." He has also been described by former United States Congressman Dick Armey as "obviously more stupid than anyone can be by accident."

Truth teller and showman, troublemaker and filmmaker, Spike Lee has been at the forefront of African-American, and indeed, of American culture for nearly a quarter of a century. How did he come to assume this role? How was he able to break down the doors of Hollywood for himself and for other African-American directors, actors, and technicians? How has he continued to grow and develop as a filmmaker? In other words, how did Spike Lee become Spike Lee as we know him today?

2

"A Very Tough Baby"

As with any artist, to understand Spike Lee, you need to understand his work. In many ways, his films *are* his life. The films that he has chosen to make—always reflecting his interests, ideas, and concerns; changing as he changes; maturing as he matures—tell the story of Spike Lee in ways that simply reciting the bare facts of his life can ever do. Before we can learn about his films, though, we need to learn about his family, his childhood, and the path he took to become one of America's most important filmmakers.

It seems strangely fitting that the family of Spike Lee, one of America's most prominent African Americans, a man who has made his career examining the African-American experience on film, can trace its ancestral line back to that of African kings. Indeed, the Lees trace their family's origins to the romance between a man who has come to be known as Mike (his African name remains unknown), the son of an African king who had been sold into slavery, and Phoebe (her African name is also lost to history), who was stolen out of her mother's arms at the age of nine and shipped to the Americas. Mike and Phoebe met in South Carolina at the turn of the nineteenth century, married, and had 11 children over the course of a 40-year marriage.

William James "Willie" Edwards, Spike Lee's great-grandfather, was born with a crippling bone disease and was not expected to live past infancy. He not only survived but defied the odds and learned to walk. Neither his illness nor a painful stuttering problem prevented him from attending the Tuskegee Institute, at the time the nation's most prominent black college. In 1893 he graduated as the class salutatorian and became a protégé of Tuskegee's founder, Booker T. Washington. Seeing the need for a similar school in his home region, the southeast corner of Alabama, Edwards returned home and opened the Snow Hill Institute. The school opened in 1893 as the Colored Literary and Industrial School in a one-room log cabin with just three students. It ultimately grew to include 27 buildings, a staff of 35, and more than 500 students, before closing in 1973.

William Edwards's drive to succeed was also evident in one of his grandchildren, Bill Lee. Born in Snow Hill in 1928, Bill attended Morehouse College in Atlanta, Georgia, with Martin Luther King Jr., who later emerged as America's greatest civil rights leader. Bill's passion was music. After mastering the acoustic double bass, he became an accomplished jazz musician, performing with such greats as Sarah Vaughan, Carmen McRae, Billie Holiday, and Duke Ellington. While at Morehouse, Bill Lee met Jacquelyn Shelton, a student at nearby Spelman College, and they married after graduation. Bill and Jacqueline were anxious to start a family. On March 20, 1957, their first son, Shelton Jackson Lee, who would become known to the world as Spike, was born in Atlanta, Georgia.

Spike Lee's father, Bill Lee, was an accomplished jazz musician well known for his proficiency on the stand-up bass. Here, Lee is shown with Judy Collins, one of the many professional musicians for whom he provided backup.

Two years later, the Lees headed north to Chicago, where there were far more musical opportunities. They finally settled in Brooklyn, New York. Jacquelyn Lee briefly took a teaching job at Saint Ann's School in Brooklyn Heights before retiring to raise her growing family, while Bill continued his musical career.

Some of Spike Lee's most vivid and cherished childhood memories are of the times his father went out on concert gigs. Spike took great pride in seeing his father onstage with leading folksingers like Odetta, Judy Collins, and Peter, Paul, and Mary. When Spike attended the gigs, he often declared to the people seated near him, "That's my father up there." During his childhood years, Spike himself took piano, guitar, and violin lessons.

Spike had no desire to follow in his father's footsteps, however. In fact, not pursuing a musical career was part of his rebellious personality. Although he appreciated jazz, he was actually a fan of the latest Motown hits by the Supremes and the Temptations, as well as leading rockers such as the Beatles—something he knew drove his father crazy: "[My father] didn't want that 'bad' music up in the house, so I had to listen to it at a very low volume or just wait till he wasn't around."

Bill Lee knew that, even if his eldest son did not become a musician, the grounding in music would benefit him, as well as Spike's younger siblings: Joie, David, Chris, Cinque, and Arnold. As Bill Lee wrote in 1990, "Music is so basic there's either a right note or a wrong note. If you play two notes and they clash, it hurts your ears. A musician learns to tell right from wrong; he learns to trust his intuition. [If you] get the rhythm, that'll lead you to the truth."

These words came to be a credo for Spike. Like his father, he became an artist who was always true to both his craft and to himself, a man who refused to compromise his artistic or political beliefs in order to gain popularity or earn a fast buck. Jacquelyn Lee saw this in him when he was only four months old. She nicknamed him Spike because, she said, he was "a very tough baby."

The name stuck. Although not tall in stature or bulky in weight, Spike was the self-described "spark plug" of the neighborhood, the one who was able to round up the troops for a game of almost anything—stickball, football, softball, basketball, even roller hockey—or just to hang out. He may not have been the best athlete in the bunch or an obvious ladies' man, but he possessed a charm that attracted both men and women. This charm would come in handy when it was time for Spike to launch his film career.

Sometimes, though, that charm did not work. Some of Spike's peers resented his "little big man" personality, and there were times when bigger, tougher kids wanted to beat him up. On one occasion, two boys actually made an appointment to beat the living daylights out of him after school, but he charmed his teacher into letting him go home early, thus escaping his pursuers.

Spike also endured some face-to-face encounters with racism. While visiting his paternal grandmother in Snow Hill, Alabama, during the early 1960s, he first saw the ugliness of segregated restrooms marked "White" and "Colored." In New York City, too, racism raised its ugly head. The Lees lived in the all-white neighborhood of Cobble Hill in Brooklyn for a short time before settling into a brownstone in racially mixed Fort Greene. While in Cobble Hill, Spike was called "nigger." The experience showed him something that he still believes many people fail to realize: that racism and prejudice are not confined to the South. Lee is quoted as saying, "People always think discrimination is just in the South. But it's like Malcolm X said: 'The South begins at the Canadian border.'"

From an early age, Spike and his brothers and sisters were taught by their parents what it meant to be African American in the United States. In the book *Spike Lee: That's My Story and I'm Sticking to It*, Lee recalled that "from early on, my parents were telling me how it was, all the time. We were always encouraged to question stuff we read in the papers or saw on TV."

These discussions became a reality as young Spike began to encounter racism for the first time: "I wanted to join the Boy

Scouts in Cobble Hill and they told me that I couldn't join because I wasn't Catholic. But really they just didn't want a black kid in the Scouts. My father sat down and explained it plain and simple to me."

Other factors also helped to shape Lee's combative personality. Saxophonist Branford Marsalis, who appeared in Lee's second film, *School Daze*, once expressed the opinion that, along with his experiences with racism, Lee's slight build and his struggle with the same stuttering problem that afflicted his great-grandfather made him distrustful of people. Bill Lee also once said of his son, "I think Spike's size has had a lot to do with his determination to do something big."

Spike also had a complex relationship with his mother. A strict disciplinarian, Jacquelyn Lee was viewed as "the bad cop" in the household, whereas Bill Lee was "the good cop." "All of us liked our father better because there was never any static coming from him," Spike Lee later explained. "It would be like, 'Daddy, can we jump off the building?' 'Yeah, go ahead.'"

Although the Lee children were not really aware of it, their middle-class lifestyle was on shaky ground. Bill Lee could be just as hardheaded as his forefathers; when the electric bass became popular in the late 1960s and 1970s, he refused to take it up, instead clinging to the traditional acoustic bass and its purer, richer sound. Because of this stance, he worked less and less, which forced Jacquelyn to return to work teaching English at Saint Ann's to help pick up the slack. "We weren't starving but sometimes it was hand-to-mouth," Lee recalled. The family may have struggled financially, but it is obvious that Bill Lee's refusal to compromise his artistic integrity no matter the cost must have had a profound effect on Lee's own career as a film director.

Unlike his siblings, who attended Saint Ann's School, Spike went to public school: John Dewey High School in Coney Island, one of New York's poorest neighborhoods. Spike dreamed of becoming a professional athlete, but as his classmate Earl Smith explained in *Spike Lee: That's My Story and I'm Sticking to It,* those dreams were unlikely to become a reality: "The funny thing is that Spike wasn't the best athlete, but he would always be captain. I guess if you're captain and choosing sides, you're always going to play. So he would grab the ball first."

Spike was not the best student, either. He hated math and science and generally did just enough to get through to the next grade. He did enjoy English though, especially his junior high encounter with *The Autobiography of Malcolm X: As Told to Alex Haley.* This book, written by Alex Haley between 1964 and 1965 and based on interviews conducted shortly before Malcolm X's death, tells the story of Malcolm X's life and ideas in his own words. The autobiography, named one of the 10 most important nonfiction books of the twentieth century by *Time* magazine, had a profound effect on Lee, who later said the autobiography was "the most important book I'll ever read." He continued, "It changed the way I thought; it changed the way I acted. It has given me courage that I didn't know I had inside me. I'm one of hundreds of thousands whose life was changed for the better." Nearly 20 years after reading it, Spike was able to combine his love for the book and his love of film to make one of his most important films.

DISCOVERING HIS PASSION

In 1975, when Spike Lee left home to attend Morehouse College (becoming the third-generation male of his family to attend that prestigious school), he had no intentions of studying film, although he did have a passion for watching them. In fact, when he entered college, he had no clear idea of what he wanted to do with his life. He took classes, began to write for the Morehouse student paper, *The Maroon Tiger,* and began to hang out with students who had interests in the performing artists.

He became friends with fellow student Monty Ross, with whom he had long, passionate discussions about politics and film. They spent many nights hanging out on the front porch of the house where Spike's grandmother Zimmie Shelton lived. Her home was just blocks from the school and she was always glad to make the friends a home-cooked meal.

Spike's grandmother did more than keep him well fed, as Spike related in *Spike Lee: That's My Story and I'm Sticking to It*: "It was my grandmother who put me through Morehouse, then NYU Film School, plus she gave me additional funds for my films at film school—the aborted *Messenger* and *She's Gotta Have It*. She wasn't rich at all—she just saved her social security checks and gave it to her struggling first grandchild."

Spike became more and more involved in the film and arts community at Morehouse. A mutual friend of Ross's and Lee's, George Folkes, helped them put together a project with assistance from the City Bureau of Cultural Arts in Atlanta to make a film. Lee wrote the screenplay, Folkes starred, and Ross directed. The film apparently was a disaster, but it was enough to encourage Lee to continue exploring film. By the time the movie was screened (no copy is known to exist), Lee had written another screenplay, entitled *It's Homecoming*. (This screenplay became the basis for his second feature film, *School Daze*.) Spike now knew what he wanted to do.

"I decided to be a filmmaker between my sophomore and junior years at Morehouse," Lee said in *Spike Lee: That's My Story and I'm Sticking to It*. "Before I left for the summer of 1977, my advisor told me I really had to declare a major when I came back, because I'd used all my electives in my first two years. I went back to New York and I couldn't find a job. There were none to be had. And that previous Christmas someone gave me a Super-8 camera, so I just started to shoot stuff."

That same summer was also one of tragedy. His mother, Jacquelyn Shelton Lee, died of liver cancer. Lee was just 19. Despite his childhood conflicts with his mother, he recognized that she had had a great deal to do with shaping his career. She had never urged him to become a filmmaker, but she had

Spike Lee is pictured here during an interview in 1991. From the beginning of his film career at New York University (NYU), Lee made films
that were controversial in their subject matter and tone.

taken him and his younger siblings to the movies religiously,
and he was enthralled with the images he saw. "She inspired
me to write," Lee later reflected. "I got my drive from her. I
think she'd like the movies I'm doing." He added, though, that
he is "not a classic case where I saw one film and decided right
then that I wanted to be a filmmaker at a young age."

Lee majored in mass communications at Morehouse. Even
if he was not yet certain that making movies would be his
ultimate calling, it was becoming obvious that he had a gift
for telling stories that had not been told before. His first film
was a 45-minute documentary entitled *Last Hustle in Brooklyn*.
The film was shot on location that summer of 1977, during
a scorching heat wave that led to a citywide power failure, or
blackout, that lasted almost 24 hours. Lee interspersed scenes

of people enjoying themselves at block parties with scenes of people stealing merchandise from Harlem stores. The title of the film played on two meanings of the word *hustle*: the dance and the art of making it any way one can—even if that meant looting. (It is interesting to note that other events in New York that summer later became, *Summer of Sam,* another feature film for Lee. It also seems likely that, when Spike saw the footage of looting in the aftermath of Hurricane Katrina, he thought back to that first film.)

Lee made other films at Morehouse, including the first one he wrote himself, *Black College: The Talented Tenth.* Lee later dismissed the movie as "a corny love story at a black campus." Despite this, he became more certain that he wanted to make movies. Even his instructor, Dr. Herb Eichelberger, however, had doubts about the likelihood of Lee succeeding as a filmmaker. After all, in 1979, very few African Americans had successfully become filmmakers. "You could only think of a few people who were black filmmakers—Oscar Micheaux, Gordon Parks, Melvin Van Peebles," Eichelberger recalled, quoted in *Spike Lee: That's My Story and I'm Sticking to It.* "But Spike was in a group that said, 'Hey I want to make some changes.'" No one who knew him then could ever have imagined the changes that Lee would make.

When Lee graduated from Morehouse in 1979, he was serious enough about filmmaking to enter the Graduate Film School at New York University (NYU). Attending the school was (and still is) viewed by many in the industry as an important first step in becoming a serious filmmaker. NYU's most famous graduate at the time was Martin Scorsese, the acclaimed director of films such as *Mean Streets, Raging Bull, Taxi Driver,* and more recently of *The Aviator* and the Academy Award–winning film *The Departed.*

Lee, however, was not drawn by the prestige associated with the school. For him, the decision to attend NYU rather than the University of Southern California (USC) or the University of California at Los Angeles (UCLA), schools with equally renowned film departments, was purely practical: He needed to be in New York City. "There's no way I could have made [my] films . . . if I lived in L.A. 'cause I didn't know anybody," he reflected. "I couldn't have called people for locations. I didn't have the resources you need to make them. You had to have an astronomical score on the GREs [Graduate Record Examination, a standard test for graduate school admission]. Also, at USC and UCLA, not everybody makes a film; the teachers assign by committee who gets to. [And] I couldn't drive." (Los Angeles is such a car-oriented city that it is nearly impossible to get around if one does not drive.)

During his first year at NYU, Lee made *The Answer*, a film that immediately labeled him a troublemaker. *The Answer* was his response to one of the most controversial movies in cinema history, D.W. Griffith's 1915 epic *The Birth of a Nation*. Griffith's film has long been admired for its artistic scope and for the use of innovative filmmaking techniques that changed the face of cinema. It has also been condemned for depicting African Americans as little more than animalistic, murderous rapists and for glorifying the activities of the Ku Klux Klan, a Southern group that often terrorized blacks. When *The Birth of a Nation* opened, the National Association for the Advancement of Colored People (NAACP) and other black organizations called on all Americans to denounce and boycott the film, but individuals as respected as President Woodrow Wilson christened it a masterpiece. After a White House screening, Wilson purportedly said, "It's like writing history with lightning. And my only regret is that it is all terribly true." Griffith's film polarized the country, led to race riots, and was partly responsible for the birth of "race" movies (films created by and starring African Americans) in the 1920s.

In Lee's *The Answer*, a black screenwriter is hired to write and direct a $50 million remake of *The Birth of a Nation* and must grapple with the dilemmas that arise from such a racially charged project. Lee included clips of Griffith's film, pointing out the despicable manner in which the black characters were portrayed. He knew that there would be a strong reaction to *The Answer*. That was, after all, the reason he did it—to provoke a response. "I knew they [his professors and fellow students] wouldn't like it," he explained. "I mean, the attitude was, 'How *dare* I denigrate the father of cinema, D. W. Griffith!'" As Lee pointed out, "I mean, it's fine to teach the great cinematic techniques that Griffith came up with. But let's not leave out the fact that that film was used as a recruiting tool for the Ku Klux Klan and was directly responsible for hundreds of black men being lynched and/or castrated."

The Answer received a poor grade, jeopardizing Lee's future at NYU. "They said that I didn't know film grammar, that the film was no good," he recalled. "The first year at NYU is probation period for everybody, so they tried to kick me out. . . . I didn't make movies that were cute and simple and safe. . . . So I knew that going [to the school], I had to try to be ten times better than my fellow white classmates."

He planned to succeed, but only on his own terms. He managed to survive that first year and went on to win a teaching assistantship during his second. With Ernest Dickerson, the only other black student in his class (who would become his cinematographer), he continued to make the type of films he wanted. After making *Sarah*, a poignant look

IN HIS OWN WORDS...

When asked about his motivation for making a film, Spike Lee said,

All directors are storytellers, so that motivation was to tell the story I wanted to tell. That's what I love.

at a family in Harlem celebrating Thanksgiving (his grand-mother had asked him to make a film that *she* would like), Lee and Dickerson produced Lee's third-year thesis, *Joe's Bed-Stuy Barbershop: We Cut Heads.* Made with just $10,000 of his grandmother's money, the film told the story of Zacha-riah Homer, a barber who gets caught up in the numbers racket (an illegal gambling scheme that has long been a fixture in some black communities). Numbers runners use Homer's shop for some of their activities, and he finally has to decide whether or not to become involved himself. His choice affects not only his life but the lives of his family and friends as well.

The Academy of Motion Picture Arts and Sciences, the organization that awards the Oscars for feature films, was so impressed with *Joe's Bed-Stuy Barbershop* that they gave it a student Academy Award. Some people were surprised, but not Lee. "NYU is one of the best film schools, and I know that [*Joe's Bed-Stuy*] was as good or better than anything [done at] USC or UCLA."

Despite graduating from NYU in 1982 with an Oscar tucked under his arm, Lee found that the doors to the Hollywood studios did not open up in the way that he and others thought they would. Like his other classmates, he was approached by big talent agencies such as William Morris and ICM, but no concrete business deals were made. "They [the agencies] said, 'We'd like to represent you. We think you're talented and we think we can help you.'" After he began to promote his origi-nal screenplay for *It's Homecoming*, which would eventually become *School Daze*, the interest disappeared. "I never got one offer, not even an 'Afterschool Special.' And there were a lot of my classmates who didn't even win Academy Awards who did get 'Afterschool Specials.'"

Lee knew that his being passed over and ignored was partly a result of race, but that did not stop him. It just motivated him more to prove his worth as a filmmaker. If he could not count on the industry gatekeepers to help him, he would have to do it himself. It would take took four years of struggle, four years of hard work, four years of scraping by and begging for funds—but he did it.

3

Spike's Gotta Make It

Making a movie is different from almost any other art form. All a writer needs is something to write with, be it pen and paper, typewriter, or computer. All a painter needs is paint and something to paint on. It costs relatively little to get started. Making a film is different. With equipment and film, actors, and other production costs, making a movie requires money and lots of it. For most aspiring filmmakers, finding a way to finance and make a movie is a major stumbling block. It was no different for Spike Lee.

Lee's first attempt at a full-length feature, *The Messenger*, was conceived as a simple story about a Brooklyn bike messenger who is the breadwinner for his family. Lee had applied to the Screen Actors Guild for an experimental film waiver, a grant awarded to independent filmmakers to offset costs for films under a certain budget. Considering his credentials and his student Academy Award, he had every reason to expect approval.

During the summer of 1984, however, when *The Messenger* had been in the preproduction (or planning) stage for eight weeks and with $20,000 of his grandmother's money already spent, the guild rejected Lee's application. The guild's review committee labeled the film "too commercial," but Lee was convinced that the true reason for the decision was racial—the film itself and the crew that worked on it were too black.

He had no choice but to shut down the project, and that put him in a very precarious position. If he gained a reputation as someone who was not able to get a film off the ground, who would want to work with him?

At the time, Lee was devastated at the failure to get *The Messenger* off the ground and at the loss of his grandmother's money. In retrospect, though, he felt that it worked out for him in the long run. In *Spike Lee: That's My Story and I'm Sticking to It*, he said,

> Nothing could prepare me for failure. At the time I thought my career was over. But in retrospect, it was the best thing that happened to me, because even if I'd got the money to make *The Messenger*, there was no way I could ever pull it off. I was not ready to do that film. It would have been a disaster, maybe something that I wouldn't have been able to rebound from. My self-confidence would have been shot.

Lee knew that, in order to save his filmmaking credibility, he would have to come up with a script for a film that could be made with as little money as possible, but still be as commercial as possible. The goal was to make a film that he himself would pay to see. As he told his friend Monty Ross, quoted in *Spike Lee*, "I'm going to give people what they want. The next script is going to have sex in it. I'm going to do something that's gonna be simple but still have integrity. And I'm going to go all the way to Hollywood." Little did he know that his film would make him a household name.

SHE'S GOTTA HAVE IT

During the fall and winter of 1984, Lee wrote the screenplay for *She's Gotta Have It*. When production began on the film the following summer, Lee and his crew of actors and production people not only created a commercially successful film, they also revitalized the independent film movement and, above all, presented African Americans with a slice of life that was more authentic and positive than anything produced in Hollywood in almost 20 years.

To say that black Americans have not fared well in Hollywood films would be an understatement. The title of Donald Bogle's 1973 classic history of black images in cinema sums up the traditional Hollywood view of black Americans: *Toms, Coons, Bucks, Mammies, and Mulattoes*. From the early days of silent film until recent times, black characters as portrayed in movies have traditionally fallen into five basic types. The first "type" is the shuffling Tom who happily does the bidding of whites without complaint. There is the grinning, singing, dancing clown (the coon) who is born to entertain the white man. There is also the sex-crazed buck; the docile female caretaker-maidservant (mammy), always there to lend support to the film's white hero or heroine; and finally, the tragic mulatto, confused because he or she is of mixed blood and is uncertain of his or her place in society.

Seen as a whole, these images made African Americans appear nonthreatening to whites (with the possible exception of the buck). By essentially stripping the characters of any degree of individuality or humanity, filmmakers reduced African Americans to easy-to-dismiss stereotypes that were acceptable to white audiences of the time.

Of course, not all African Americans agreed to accept the roles assigned to them, and several individuals arose to challenge these stereotypes, among them Oscar Micheaux. Beginning in the 1920s, Micheaux produced, wrote, and directed

In *She's Gotta Have It*, Spike Lee's first feature film, Tracy Camilla Johns plays Nola Darling, a well-educated young black woman who is being courted by three different men. Johns is pictured here in a scene from the film with Tommy Redmond Hicks, who played Jamie Overstreet, one of Nola's suitors.

a number of films that explored the reality and diversity of African-American life. Called "race movies," Micheaux's films ran the gamut of film genres, including romance, adventure, comedy, drama, and mystery. The films presented black men and women as heroes and villains, professionals and laborers, and even sex symbols. Prominent artists such as Paul Robeson got their start in race films, and their popularity with black audiences led to the rise of a completely separate, or segregated, black-owned movie theater industry.

Wishing to tap the growing black audience that flocked to race movies, Hollywood also attempted to tackle black themes through a different dramatic formula. Hollywood studios produced a number of "message" films between the late 1940s and the mid-1960s. Films such as *Pinky* in 1949, *The Defiant Ones* in 1958, and *Guess Who's Coming to Dinner?* in 1967 explored what was then called the "race problem." The makers of these films attempted to present black characters in more complex situations than had previously been seen in Hollywood films and to show them as "real" people. Although the situations were serious, the films were almost always resolved in a slightly unbelievable fashion, ending on a note of superficial racial harmony. Moreover, none of these films allowed black characters to live in a world of their own; they were generally shown struggling for a spot in white society, suggesting that there was nothing attractive about the black community.

Race movies, on the other hand, celebrated black community life. Still, the best intentions of black filmmakers could not hold out against the more polished look and appeal of big-budget Hollywood films, which began to attract the big-name talent that black audiences wanted to see, including stars such as Lena Horne and Ethel Waters. As a result, the race movie industry was mostly dead by the mid 1950s.

Black audiences who hoped that Hollywood would finally grant black characters true dramatic freedom continued to be disappointed. In fact, in the period between the demise of the race movie and the advent of black exploitation films in the 1970s, the two films that treated black characters with sensitivity were not big studio films, but rather independently produced projects: *Nothing But a Man* (1965) and *The Learning Tree* (1969).

Nothing But a Man and *The Learning Tree* were well received by both critics and black audiences. The former became an art-house staple, resurfacing in early 1993 on video. The latter has become a love letter to and for African Americans who grew up in rural areas. The class and integrity of these films were lost on Hollywood, however. The studios blasted into the 1970s with blaxploitation films, in which hip, street-smart ghetto dwellers finally got the chance to defeat the "pigs" (police officers) and "honkies" (white people in general) who had always beaten them down. With colorful titles such as *Superfly, Cleopatra Jones, Black Belt Jones, Foxy Brown* and *Blacula* (Hollywood's version of a black Dracula), these films were aimed at a black audience hungry to see themselves on screen—along with curious whites—and provided them with fantastic superheroes who could defeat any white man and heat up the screen with their sex appeal.

Roles for black actors may have been more available in the blaxploitation era, but the characters were still two-dimensional and cartoonlike. In addition, few opportunities arose for black writers, producers, and directors; almost all of the blaxploitation films were conceived and created by whites. Only two blacks worked consistently behind the camera in the 1970s: Michael Schultz, who directed lightweight comedy fare such as *Car Wash* and *Which Way Is Up?* and Sidney Poitier, who directed a series of films starring himself, including *Buck and the Preacher, A Piece of the Action,* and *Let's Do It Again.*

When *She's Gotta Have It* entered theaters in limited release in 1986, it picked up where films like *Nothing But a Man* and *The Learning Tree* left off. In his first feature film, Spike Lee had written, edited, directed, and costarred in a comedy-drama that had an all-black cast and told a kind of story in which blacks had never before been featured.

The "she" of the title is Nola Darling (Tracy Camilla Johns), an artist in her 20s who lives in the Fort Greene section of Brooklyn. Nola, a sexually liberated woman, is torn among the three men in her life: Jamie Overstreet (Tommy Redmond Hicks), a humble, lovelorn gentleman; Greer Childs (John Canada Terrell), a snobby, muscle-bound male model; and Mars Blackmon—an unemployed "homeboy" (street hood) who wears high-top sneakers, a giant necklace with his name on it, and thick-framed glasses—played by Spike Lee himself. Why did Lee cast himself in such a pivotal role? Simple economics—he didn't have the money to hire anyone else.

Nola is a direct challenge to a society that expects women to be submissive and ready to settle down, while men are encouraged to be sexually aggressive. In *She's Gotta Have It*, the roles are reversed. Nola expects the men in her life to be there for her when she wants them. She is the one who decides when Jamie, Greer, and Mars can see her, how they can see her, and for how long. This is what makes the three men so uncomfortable; Nola is in control—not only of herself, but of them as well. The traditional roles have been reversed, and none of the men in Nola's life are in the least bit happy about it. Any film with such a plot would probably have raised eyebrows, but the fact that the principal characters were African American made it revolutionary.

Less than 90 minutes long, *She's Gotta Have It* was shot on the streets of Brooklyn in a mere 12 days. The film's total budget was only $175,000; the average cost of a studio film during this period was $18 million. The lack of money shows in the final product, but Lee used every directing and editing trick in the book to help disguise the film's low budget.

Even with such a low budget, coming up with the funds to make the movie was a constant struggle. The money did not come all at once in one big check, but instead came in a little at a time. Lee remembers anxiously waiting for the mailman to come every day, hoping he was bringing good news—more money. Lee even used his own money to cover expenses, and at one point his phone and electricity were shut off because he could not pay the bills. There were even times when the crew members used the deposits from their empty soda bottles and cans to buy film stock.

Lee had no qualms about approaching perfect strangers for funds. He set up screenings for investors at his alma mater, NYU, to help finish the film and sought out the support of black media professionals and artists in the city, such as Nelson George, then the soul music critic and columnist for *Billboard* magazine. Lee screened a few reels of *She's Gotta Have It* in George's apartment one evening, and George knew he had no choice but to help. "I'd never seen anything like it," he wrote in the introduction to Lee's first movie companion book, *Spike Lee's Gotta Have It*. He was struck by the film's links with the works of directors such as Oscar Micheaux. "[Those] film hustlers beat the odds to reach theaters with pictures that reflected their views of what Blacks wanted to see," George wrote. "Spike, in their tradition, did the same."

She's Gotta Have It portrays a black world from start to finish, from Nola's community (the viewer is treated to photo-essays of Fort Greene's parks, playgrounds, and brownstones) to the apartment she lives in. Among her decorations are a shrine dedicated to Malcolm X, whose birth date (May 19) she shares, and a collage of newspaper clippings dedicated to victims of police brutality and racial violence in the city. Scenes such as the one in which Nola greases Mars's scalp present everyday rituals with which black audiences could easily identify.

DID YOU KNOW?

Spike Lee created two retail companies: Spike's Joint, which was based in the Fort Greene section of Brooklyn, and Spike's Joint West, in Los Angeles. Both stores, which sold hats, T-shirts, postcards, and other memorabilia from Spike's films, closed in 1997, so that Lee could concentrate his energies on filmmaking.

Lee knew he had a winner on his hands with *She's Gotta Have It*, but he also knew that completing the film was just half the battle. He now faced the task of getting the right people to see it and having the right studio pick it up.

Positive buzz had already begun about the project before its legendary premiere at the San Francisco International Film Festival in the spring of 1986. Halfway through the screening, the theater was darkened by a power outage, but the audience was so engrossed with the film that they refused to leave. Lee was asked to go up on stage and answer questions, his face illuminated by a flashlight. The police arrived and advised everyone to evacuate, but right after that announcement the power was restored and the screening continued.

The film's run of good fortune continued. After its success in San Francisco, a contingent of studios began to bid against each other for the right to distribute it. The so-called major studios, such as Columbia, Universal Studios, 20th Century Fox, and Paramount Pictures were not involved, but their absence did not bother Lee at all. He felt that the major studios would not know how to handle and market his small, African-American–oriented film. "We didn't want to go to the big ones," he said. After entertaining offers from Circle Films, the Samuel Goldwyn Company, and Orion Pictures, Lee settled on Island Pictures because of its record of success in promoting small films. The company had just enjoyed a major success with *Kiss of the Spider Woman* and was hungry to build on its reputation for high-quality independent films. Lee was also pleased with Island's response to *She's Gotta Have It*: "They saw it for what it was—a black film—and didn't want to disguise that fact. They were not afraid of having a film that would have a majority black audience."

Island and Lee kept their deal secret until after the summer, when *She's Gotta Have It* had its international premiere at the most prestigious of all film events—the Cannes Film Festival. The film was an immense hit, winning the Prix de la Jeunesse for Best New Film. Although pleased, Lee was disappointed that the film did not also win the Camera d'Or for Outstanding First Feature. Claiming "we wuz robbed," Lee angered many reporters, who felt that the new director had a bit of an attitude. It would not be the last time that Lee alienated members of the press.

Even still, glowing articles about him began to appear in major publications such as the *Washington Post.* As media attention grew, Island Pictures announced that *She's Gotta Have It* would begin an exclusive engagement on August 15, 1986, at just one venue, the Cinema Studio in Manhattan. By opening the film at a single theatre, the company made the opening "an event," adding to the word of mouth already building around the film.

The result of Island's marketing strategy was enough to make Lee weep for joy: people lined up around the block to see his movie. In order to savor the public's enthusiasm, Lee himself often stood outside the theater, handing out free *She's Gotta Have It* buttons and selling T-shirts and postcards— anything to bring an audience to his film.

Although they recognized the historical importance of *She's Gotta Have It,* the critics were restrained in their praise. The *New York Post* dubbed Lee "the black Woody Allen." Allen is another New York filmmaker; he is famous for his urban romantic comedies. This comparison that did not sit well with Lee, who failed to see what he and Allen (who is Jewish) had in common, except that they were both short and wore glasses. The *New York Daily News* complained that Tracy Camilla Johns did not have the sex appeal, "à la Marilyn Monroe," for the kind of role she was cast in. Lee responded:

> I purposely cast the role of Nola with a dark-skinned-look-
> ing black woman with natural hair because I wanted to show
> how diverse the beauty is in the black community. [Those
> critics] would've been more comfortable if [Tracy] looked

like Lena Horne or Dorothy Dandridge. But, contrary to the media, beauty does not only mean light skin, light eyes, and light hair. It comes in all shades and shapes, and Tracy proved that.

Critics made similar observations about Jamie, Greer, and Mars. One reviewer claimed that "they were types [of black men] one wouldn't normally happen across." Nelson George, the *Billboard* critic, laughed at this notion. "They were real Black men, not the commercial garbage spewed out of a White Hollywood writer's Negro-cliché processor," George asserted. "It was no surprise that the film would be judged by White values and tastes. But to really understand and respect

Dorothy Dandridge

Of all the stories of the African-American performers whose lives and careers were harmed by racism, few are as tragic as that of Dorothy Dandridge (November 9, 1922–September 8, 1965).

Dandridge began performing in nightclubs as a little girl. As a teenager, she appeared in small roles in a number of films. When she married Harold Nicholas in 1945, she virtually retired from performing. After her divorce in 1951, Dandridge returned to performing in nightclubs, where she came face to face with the racism that was still a part of everyday life. When performing at a hotel in Las Vegas, for example, she was only allowed to do her act; she was forbidden to talk with patrons or to use of any of the hotel facilities, such as the elevator, lobby, swimming pool, or public bathrooms.

Despite these difficulties, Dandridge became an international star, singing in Paris, London, Rio de Janeiro, San Francisco, and New York. Making it in Hollywood, however, proved more difficult. After appearing in such forgettable films as *Tarzan's Peril* and *The Harlem Globetrotters*, she had her first major role in *Bright Road* (1953), playing a schoolteacher opposite Harry Belafonte.

Her next role, the lead in *Carmen Jones* (1954)—a film adaptation of the Bizet opera *Carmen*—made her a star. A strikingly beautiful and talented woman, she became the first African American to earn an Academy Award nomination for Best Actress. Although she lost to Grace Kelly, she became its point of view, you had to stretch and see where it was coming from."

Not all the complaints came from white reviewers, however. Some of *She's Gotta Have It*'s most vocal critics turned out to be African-American women. Although they were happy that the film celebrated black life, some of the women did not agree that Nola's free-spirited sexual expression made her a liberated woman. Actress Abiola Sinclair, a columnist for New York's black weekly newspaper, the *Amsterdam News*, felt that the film endorsed the idea that black women are by nature sexually promiscuous.

Others argued that Lee "had a problem" with black women, an accusation that has followed him throughout his career.

a famous movie star and even appeared on the cover of *Life* magazine. She seemed poised to become the first black actress to have the kind of career and success that only white actresses had achieved.

Unfortunately, it was not to be. In the years that followed *Carmen Jones*, Dandridge was unable to find film roles that suited her talents. Hollywood filmmakers were at a loss on how to use the light-skinned actress, who soon found herself appearing in a series of poorly received dramas such as *Tamango* and *Malaga*. Unable to cope with her struggling career and the failure of her second marriage, to Jack Denison, Dandridge began to drink heavily and to take antidepressants.

Forced to resume her nightclub act, Dandridge was unable to resurrect her career and found herself appearing in second-rate lounges and stage productions. She soon suffered a nervous breakdown, and, on September 8, 1965, she was found dead of an apparent suicide.

Forgotten for many years, her tragic life became the subject of interest again in the 1990s, when Halle Berry won a Golden Globe award for her performance in the HBO movie *Introducing Dorothy Dandridge*. Through Berry's remarkable performance, a new generation was introduced to a highly talented woman whose career was tragically cut short because of the lack of opportunity for African-American actors in the 1950s.

Nola, in their eyes, was not truly independent because she relied on men to fulfill her needs. They believed that what she sought in others she should have found in herself. Lee was perplexed by these reactions, but he understood why people were moved to criticize his film: "Look, not that many black films get made every year, and when they are, everyone is expecting to see themselves, and when they don't see the image *they* want to see, they get uptight. But, I have no hate for black women or black men, and I don't see that in the film. I think I was fair to everyone."

These controversies did nothing to slow the momentum of *She's Gotta Have It*. Indeed, despite the film's flaws, it was obvi-

Forty Acres and a Mule

Spike Lee's production company, 40 Acres & A Mule Filmworks, was named for the compensation that was thought to be given to freed slaves after the Civil War—40 acres of land to farm and a mule to work the land. The true story behind the phrase, though, is slightly more complicated.

As Union soldiers advanced through the South, the problem of what should be done for the freed slaves arose. On January 16, 1865, Major General William T. Sherman issued Special Field Order No. 15, which applied *only* to black families who lived near the coasts of South Carolina, Georgia, and Florida. It granted each freed family 40 acres of tillable land on islands and the coast of Georgia. There was no promise of mules, but a number of surplus mules were also granted to settlers.

By June 1865, approximately 40,000 freed slaves had been settled on 400,000 acres in Georgia and South Carolina, and news of "40 acres and a mule" spread quickly throughout the South, raising hopes that all former slaves would receive the same compensation. Andrew Johnson, however, who assumed the office of president after the assassination of President Abraham Lincoln, revoked Sherman's orders, which had only applied to three states in the first place, and returned the land to its white owners. Because of this, the phrase "40 acres and a mule" has come to symbolize the government's broken promises and failure to help African Americans recover from the legacy of slavery.

Spike Lee's character in *She's Gotta Have It*, Mars Blackmon, became so popular that Lee was asked to reprise the role in a series of commercials with Michael Jordan (left) for Nike. Lee also directed the commercials.

ous that a new and exciting voice in cinema had been found. The film went into national distribution that October and racked up more than $8 million in box office receipts, making it one of the most successful independent films ever made. Lee suddenly found himself in demand. He appeared on the *Today* show, received an offer to direct a music video for jazz legend Miles Davis's new album (*Tutu*), and appeared on NBC's *Saturday Night Live* with rap group Run-D.M.C. He officially set up his own filmworks company in Fort Greene and named it 40 Acres & a Mule. Three of Lee's family members would also become a part of the 40 Acres group after proving themselves in *She's Gotta Have It*: his sister, Joie (who played Nola's ex-roommate, Clorinda Bradford); his father (who played Nola's father and composed the music for the film); and his brother Cinque (who worked as a production assistant).

For all his newfound fame, Lee had to share the spotlight with his cinematic alter ego, Mars Blackmon, the most popular character in the film. Mars' tag line—"Please baby, please baby, please"—became a catchphrase for many urban young people. Realizing the appeal of the character, Nike signed Lee to direct a commercial featuring Mars and a man Lee admired: Chicago Bulls star Michael Jordan. The pairing of Lee and Jordan kicked off one of the most culturally and financially successful ad campaigns of all time.

While Island basked in the glow of helping Lee make history, several studios began to jockey for the chance to release what would be his first studio-financed feature film. Lee dusted off his college-era script for *It's Homecoming* and prepared to prove to the world that the success of *She's Gotta Have It* was no fluke. He would soon learn firsthand what he had always suspected: Hollywood may be all glitz and glamour to the public, but it's a different matter behind the scenes.

4

Color Craze

Lee was definitely sitting on top of the world after the success of *She's Gotta Have It.* It had been 15 years since an independent black filmmaker had caught the industry's eye, and Lee was getting the opportunity to do what Melvin Van Peebles and so many other talented African-American filmmakers had been denied—the chance to make it inside the Hollywood system.

Now that he was playing in the big leagues, however, Lee had to play by big league rules. For a person who always had trouble tolerating the status quo, the experience of working on a studio-budgeted project—under studio supervision—was bound to be difficult. Things got off to a rocky start in December 1986, when Island Pictures expressed misgivings about aspects of *It's Homecoming,* now known as *School Daze.* The studio indicated that they did not have the $3 million Lee was expecting to finance the film. They tried to convince Lee and his coproducer, Monty Ross, that the film could be made for less. With preproduction on the film about to start, Ross feared that history would repeat itself. "Spike should not develop a reputation for beginning projects and then not be able to produce them because of money. We did that with *The Messenger*. There is no way we would let that happen with *School Daze*. Too much was at stake."

Ross and Lee went to work on the budget but were unable to make the necessary cuts. With negotiations leading nowhere, Island decided to drop out of the deal, leaving the filmmakers in a serious quandary. "We had already begun to audition people. We had hotels set up [in Atlanta]," Ross recalled. "Vendors [were] contacted, and cast and crew in New York and L.A. were packing their bags. The phone was ringing off the hook."

Lee and Ross needed a miracle, and they got one in the person of Columbia Pictures executive David Picker, who heard about the project while visiting New York. After reading the script, Picker flew back to Los Angeles and convinced his boss, David Puttnam, to provide backing for *School Daze*. Not only did Lee receive financial backing, he got something put in his contract that very few directors, white or black, ever receive: the right to the final cut. This means that Lee alone would have the last say regarding the final version of the film.

After dealing with the film industry powers, Lee also had to deal with the conservative administration at his alma mater, Morehouse College, where *School Daze* was to be filmed. The university officials had been reluctant to grant filming privileges, and, during the shoot, Morehouse kicked Lee and his film crew off campus grounds. The administrators had decided that *School Daze* would portray black college life and, by extension, black Americans in a negative light. Atlanta University offered its facilities, and Lee and his crew were able to finish filming on that campus.

When *School Daze* was completed, it was not hard to see why the college officials had been uncomfortable. The film, which

While a student at Morehouse College, Lee became friends with Monty Ross (above in 2007), a fellow student. Later, Ross also went into film work and collaborated with Lee on certain films, including *School Daze*.

takes place during homecoming weekend at the fictitious Mission College, tells the story of fraternity and sorority members clashing with other students and "townies." Still, *School Daze* is not just a typical college comedy. Instead, the film investigates black politics and attitudes toward apartheid in South Africa and examines one of the most closely held secrets within the black community: prejudice between light-skinned and dark-skinned blacks.

Lee used the film to highlight divisions within the black community based on class and skin color. For some students, being too black, either in color or culture, is something to be shunned. Julian (played by Giancarlo Esposito) dismisses the ideas of Dap (played by Laurence Fishburne) as "African mumbo jumbo" and laughs at his fascination with the motherland ("We are, without question, black *Americans*"). A member of the Gamma Rays, the sister organization of Gamma Phi Gamma, dismisses rap music as "hip-hop B-boy nonsense."

The students at Mission College are also divided by class lines. Dap seems to believe that anyone who wants a good job or career is a "sellout." His four homeboys, Da Fellas, think that he has allowed his quest for racial justice to overshadow the one thing that their ancestors strived for: the opportunity to become whatever or whomever one wishes to be. When Dap and Da Fellas venture off campus to a local Kentucky Fried Chicken, they are confronted by the Local Yokels, a group of local men, "townies," who are tired of out-of-town college students stealing all the jobs, women, and status. One of the Yokels, played by Samuel L. Jackson, tells them, "Y'all niggers and you gonna be niggers, forever, just like us." Dap, visibly shaken by the exchange, says, "You're not niggers." Even Dap, though, cannot ignore the

IN HIS OWN WORDS...

In an interview with Cindy Fuchs at citypaper.net, Lee reflected on racism in Hollywood:

> I want to state that Spike Lee is not saying that African-American culture is just for black people alone to enjoy and cherish. Culture is for everybody.

School Daze **is the story of homecoming weekend at Mission College, a fictitious black school. Above is a shot of the fraternity members featured in the movie. Though the film was a comedy, it also tackled serious subjects such as black politics and apartheid in South Africa.**

damage that centuries of racism have done to their self-esteem or deny the truth of their insight into white society.

School Daze also explores race and class conflicts through a variety of musical numbers. Probably its most telling tune is "Straight and Nappy." Written by Spike's father, Bill Lee, the seven-minute piece is performed in Madame Re Re's beauty salon, where two groups of women, the Jigaboos and the Wannabes, trade vicious insults. The Wannabes are light skinned with straight ("good") hair, and most wear blue contact lenses; in the eyes of the Jigaboos, they "wannabe white." The Jigaboos are dark skinned with nappy ("bad") hair; the Wannabes are convinced that the Jigaboos are jealous of them ("Don't you wish you had hair like this?/Then the boys would give you a kiss").

In this battle of the hairstyles, there are no winners. Both groups have been conditioned to despise themselves, and that self-hatred is reinforced by other blacks who toss around epithets ("pickaninny," "high-yellow heifer," and "tar baby" are just a few) that degrade the appearance of other blacks the way whites did years ago.

Thus, when Dap screams for his fellow students to "Wake up!" at the end of the film, it is a call to all African Americans to respect and nurture the African in themselves, to reject the false values that divide them along color and class lines, and to really strive toward unity. (The use of the phrase "wake up" echoes in Lee's films throughout his career.)

Although Columbia executives were pleased with the rough cut of the film, they suggested that Lee do a few screenings to see how *School Daze* tested with different audiences. Some whites found the story to be a little "too black" for them to understand, but they, like the majority of the blacks, enjoyed the way Lee wove serious racial and social issues together with comedy and music. Other audience members thought that the film was too long and confusing at times, with too many subplots and issues. By the time the screenings ended, Lee and the producers had cut *School Daze* from 2 hours and 25 minutes to a tight 1 hour and 56 minutes.

Lee's headaches were just beginning, though. David Puttnam, president of Columbia, was suddenly replaced by Dawn Steel, whom Lee did not particularly care for. Steel was said to have little interest in most of the films in which Puttnam had played a major role, and that included *School Daze*. As a result, Lee's relationship with the studio rapidly went downhill.

Columbia informed Lee that there would not be any television commercials, posters in subways, radio spots, or ads in black publications such as *Essence*, *Ebony*, or *Jet*. Lee called this move a "slap in the face to the black consumer and the black media." Instead of using tried-and-true advertising tactics, Columbia wanted to send Lee on a promotional tour that would cover 21 cities in 21 days. Lee, who was not at all happy with the idea of being worked "like a Georgia mule," drafted his own plan for a two-week tour that would start on the West Coast.

One of his first interviews was on NBC's *Today* show, where he was questioned by Bryant Gumbel, morning television's first African-American star. To Lee's and Columbia's dismay, Gumbel criticized Lee for daring to air the black community's dirty laundry in public. He was not alone in this criticism. Following the lead of the administrations of Morehouse and Spelman, other African Americans took offense at Lee's view of both black college life and the black middle class. Some critics also complained that the film's women were relegated to the occasional musical number and then pushed into the background, where, once again, their actions were influenced by the male characters.

For the nation's film critics, the majority of whom were white, *School Daze* was generally puzzling. Most praised the performances of Lee and Fishburne, but some felt that, given the serious subject matter, the story should not have been a musical comedy. Others thought that Lee was being overly ambitious with his first studio-financed feature, suggesting that he should have chosen a less complex project. Janet Maslin of the *New York Times* especially angered Lee when she called the film his "little musical." Lee accused Maslin of being condescending and patronizing—not to mention racist—for not stretching to understand the material. Finally, like many other directors, he decided to stop reading reviews altogether. He realized that, by reading reviews and trying to make the critics happy, he would not be making movies that made *him* happy.

Despite the mixed reviews, *School Daze* turned out to be one of Columbia's top-grossing films of 1988. For a mere $6.5 million investment, the studio took in $15 million. It also made history on two fronts: It was one of the least expensive musicals ever made, and it was the first with a black cast to be directed by an African American. By making a musical that examined the kind of issues not normally seen in Hollywood musicals, Lee had once again broken new ground as a filmmaker.

In the end, Lee had passed his first test as a studio director and was well on his way to going where no other black filmmaker had gone before. All he had to do was keep the momentum going. As he admitted, "No other black filmmaker has been able to go from one film to another." In order to stay in the game, though, he would have to hit a home run his next time at bat.

5

Do the Race Thing

After *School Daze*, Lee found himself in the same position he was in after his first low-budget feature, *The Messenger*, failed to take off. *School Daze* was not a flop and did actually make money, but the *perception* of the film was that it did not live up to expectations. Because of this, in some ways, Lee was right back to square one as a filmmaker, having to prove himself once again to white Hollywood.

Lee knew that was always going to be an issue, that he would constantly have to prove himself. As he said in a 1989 interview with Marlaine Glickman, published in *Spike Lee Interviews*:

> When I was becoming a filmmaker I knew it would be
> harder for me to be a black filmmaker—to be a filmmaker
> because I was black. But I realized that you just have to be
> two or three—four—times better. The same thing as any
> black athlete. They got to be better than the white boy to

make the team. You don't sit there and brood about it. This is something you just know, growing up black. It's a given. The problem starts when people say that's a given and then use that as the excuse.

He knew that his next film had to be more than just good for him to continue to have a career in Hollywood. It would have to blow away both the critics and the public. *Do the Right Thing* had all the ingredients to make that happen.

The film was inspired by a racial incident that took place in Howard Beach, an Italian-American neighborhood in Queens, New York, in December 1986. After their car broke down on the highway, a trio of black men set out on foot to get help. They stopped at a pizza parlor to eat and use a phone. Sensing that they were not welcome, they left the establishment, only to have their worst fears confirmed: A gang of bat-wielding white youths descended on them, screaming racial epithets and telling them to leave the neighborhood. The white men chased the black men for miles. One was caught and beaten, and another escaped. The third, Michael Griffith, a West Indian immigrant, ran out onto an expressway to escape his pursuers and was struck and killed by a car.

When the white youths were put on trial, their lawyers portrayed Griffith and the other two men as troublemakers who were looking for a fight (one of them apparently had a knife), pointing to their police records and Griffith's alleged cocaine use. By making the incident seem more like an ordinary brawl than a racially motivated attack, the defense prevented any of the white young men from being convicted of causing Griffith's death.

The highly publicized Howard Beach case inspired Lee to create a film that, he said, would analyze how racism affects not only the victims but the racists themselves. Having previously contemplated making a movie to be called *Heatwave*, he decided to set the action during the hottest day of the sum-

Do the Right Thing depicts a day in the life of a community in the Bedford-Stuyvesant section of Brooklyn during the summer of 1988. In the movie, Mookie (center), Spike Lee's character, is a delivery man for Sal (Danny Aiello, right of center), who owns the local pizzeria.

mer because, as he said in the book *Spike Lee: That's My Story and I'm Sticking to It*, "In New York you have eight million people on top of each other, and people get crazy when it's hot. Things start to get frayed. If you bump into someone, you might get shot."

On the surface, *Do the Right Thing* is a day in the life of a community. Shot entirely on one block in the Bedford-Stuyvesant section of Brooklyn during the summer of 1988, the film introduces viewers to a cast of characters that are classic types in many black communities. The residents include Mother Sister (Ruby Dee), who sits in her window, keeping an eye on the neighborhood; Da Mayor (Ossie Davis), the local wino who has seen a lot and has a store of knowledge to impart; the Cornermen—M.L. (Paul Benjamin), Coconut Sid (Frankie Faison), and Sweet Dick Willie (Robin Harris)—who park themselves under an umbrella on a corner and spend the day talking about anything and everything; the members of the neighborhood teen posse, who spend their Saturday "hangin' tough"; and Mister Señor Love Daddy (Samuel L. Jackson), the local disc jockey for WE LOVE radio, a storefront station.

Ossie Davis

Audiences today may know Ossie Davis best for his performances in Spike Lee films such as *Do The Right Thing* and *Jungle Fever*, but even before that, he had a long and distinguished career as an actor, director, and playwright. Davis helped to blaze a trail for other African Americans in theater and films.

Born Raiford Chatman Davis on December 18, 1917, Davis made his Broadway debut in 1946 after serving in the U.S. Army during World War II. Although Davis had made many appearances in films, plays, and television, he first became widely celebrated in 1961 for his starring performance in his own play *Purlie Victorious*, a satirical look at traditional Southern race relations. This play was also turned into a 1963 film retitled *Gone Are the Days!* and a 1970 Broadway musical, *Purlie*. Davis wrote, produced, and directed plays and films and costarred many times with his wife, actress Ruby Dee, whom he married in 1948.

Ossie Davis was also well known for his longtime political activism. He and Ruby Dee were close personal friends of Malcolm X, Jesse Jackson, and Martin Luther King Jr., and were instrumental in organizing the 1963 Civil Rights March on Washington. With Ahmed Osman, Davis delivered the eulogy at Malcolm X's funeral and later reread part of his eulogy at the end of Lee's film *Malcolm X*. He also delivered the eulogy for Martin Luther King Jr.

In 2004, Ossie Davis and Ruby Dee were honored at Washington's Kennedy Center for the Performing Arts for their lasting contribution to American culture. Davis died on February 4, 2005, of natural causes. Busy to the end, he had just finished working on the Showtime television series *The L Word* and had begun work on a film called *Retirement*. Ossie Davis, whose career spanned nearly 60 years, was an American legend whose work helped to pave the way for every African-American actor, director, and playwright who followed.

The central character, though, is Mookie (Spike Lee), a young man who has a job making deliveries for Sal's Pizzeria, an establishment that has been in the community for decades. Sal (Danny Aiello) is proud of this fact, boasting that most of the neighborhood kids "grew up on my pizza."

Everyone in the neighborhood frequents Sal's, including Radio Raheem (Bill Nunn), who storms into the joint with his ever-present boom box pumping out his (and the film's) theme song, "Fight the Power," which disses white American icons like Elvis Presley and John Wayne. A character called Buggin' Out (Giancarlo Esposito) disturbs the peace at Sal's in another way. After looking at the pictures of Italian Americans such as Frank Sinatra, Al Pacino, Joe DiMaggio, and Robert De Niro, he demands that Sal put "some brothers up on the wall," such as Michael Jordan and Nelson Mandela. Sal refuses, and Buggin' Out returns to Sal's that evening with Radio Raheem and Smiley, another neighborhood fixture. They demand African-American representation on Sal's walls while playing the music on Radio Raheem's boom box at a deafening volume. Sal, who thinks of himself as a liberal, comes face to face with his own prejudice: He screams out the word *nigger*. When Sal demolishes Radio Raheem's boom box with a baseball bat, a fight breaks out and spills out into the street. The police arrive, and, as they attempt to restrain Radio Raheem, they kill him by applying a choke hold too long. Mookie reacts by throwing a garbage can through Sal's window. A riot erupts, and the pizzeria goes up in flames. The morning after, Sal and Mookie have a verbal showdown in front of the burned-out building.

Do the Right Thing was filmed during one of the hottest summers on record in New York, and the sights and sounds of the sweltering city are vividly captured by Lee's longtime cinematographer, Ernest Dickerson. The film, which strikes a daring balance between humor and racial politics, shows the ugliness of the bigotry woven into the social fabric of the country. In one scene, five characters each look directly into the camera and rattle off a barrage of slurs about another group they have no tolerance for. By presenting this venom in such a direct manner, Lee forces viewers to see that, although they may privately laugh about racial and ethnic stereotypes, there is nothing the least bit funny about them.

Lee ends the film at a kind of crossroads, with contrasting quotes from two men of very different views who were pivotal figures during that era: Martin Luther King Jr. and Malcolm X. King's quote denounces violence: "Violence as a way of achieving racial justice is both impractical and immoral." Malcolm X, on the other hand, says, "I am not against using violence in self-defense. I don't even call it violence when it is self-defense, I call it intelligence." Audiences are left to consider which view Lee embraces and whether Mookie did in fact "do the right thing" by throwing the garbage can through Sal's window. By leaving some things uncertain, Lee forced the audience to contemplate these things for themselves. This uncertainty, the refusal to spell everything out, is part of the film's greatness, but it seemed to confuse both critics and audiences alike.

Do the Right Thing made its worldwide debut at the Cannes Film Festival. Lee, who met the press wearing the same baggy shorts, high-top sneakers, and low-cut fade (a hairstyle popular at the time) Mookie sported in the film, knew that he would have to defend himself against charges that the film was too abrasive. He probably did not count on becoming an instant expert on race. "Why aren't there many riots in New York or Chicago?" asked one journalist.

A couple of questions really got him fired up. One reporter, for example, complained that the neighborhood in *Do the Right Thing* was "too clean. . . . There's no garbage, no drugs. Where's the rape, where's the crack?" This really made Lee's blood boil: "The questions I get asked by journalists a white filmmaker would never get asked. . . . Those insights just show [people's] racist notions of how black people are. We were not going to have garbage, squalor, and broken glass, and women throwing their babies out of windows. *Do the Right Thing* is not about a ghetto. It's about racism and racism exists everywhere."

The lack of understanding about Lee's intentions and subject matter may have cost *Do the Right Thing* the Palme d'Or (Golden Palm) Award for Best Film. Lee felt that he was unfairly snubbed, and he was not alone. Actress Sally Field, a member of that year's jury, later told him, "I fought for your movie until the end, and I would do it again." Field told Lee that the other jurors "didn't like that Mookie threw the garbage can through the window. I don't think they understood it."

Lee's experience at Cannes was mild compared to the firestorm that erupted when the film was released in the United States. Most critics agreed that *Do the Right Thing* was a stunning piece of filmmaking. *Newsweek*'s David Ansen testified, "You leave the movie stunned, challenged, drained. . . . It's the funkiest and most informed view of racism an American filmmaker has given us." Roger Ebert of the *Chicago Sun-Times* called the film "an entertaining, upbeat, joyous slice of life" and picked it as the best film of the year in his annual list. The *Christian Science Monitor* went a step further, designating *Do the Right Thing* "the most important American film of the eighties."

A group of nervous commentators began to sound the alarm, however, finding the film to be, in the words of one critic, "dynamite under every seat." One of the most vocal doomsayers was Joe Klein of *New York* magazine. "Spike Lee's reckless new movie opens on . . . June 30 (in not too many theaters near you, one hopes)," he announced in his column, going on to say, "Black teenagers won't find it so hard [to figure out that] white people are [their] enemy," and, suggested that, following Mookie's lead, they would start race riots at theaters. (The charge was not new: Paramount Pictures, which had initially expressed an interest in financing the movie, backed out for this very reason.) Klein also predicted that, because of the film, David Dinkins, the Manhattan borough president, would lose his bid to become the city's first African-American mayor.

Lee countered by saying that he made *Do the Right Thing* to spark a dialogue, not a riot. "Mookie did what he did because he was angry," Lee said. "He saw for himself how the system destroys black people. What was he supposed to do: stand there and lead everybody in a chorus of 'We Are the World?'" Contrary to what Klein claimed, Lee believed that the movie would make New Yorkers see that the current mayor, Ed Koch, had done little to promote racial harmony during his 12 years as mayor and that they would vote Dinkins into office.

Some critics' reactions to *Do the Right Thing* and the controversy surrounding the film may have kept some from seeing it, but the film still became a moderate box-office hit. By year's end, it made more than $28 million, more than four times its $6.5 million budget. The film did not fare so well, however, when the year's awards were handed out. Although the Los Angeles Critics group named *Do the Right Thing* Best Picture of 1989 and awarded it honors for Best Director and Best Screenplay to Lee, all the other major critics' groups passed it over. When the Oscar nominations were announced on Valentine's Day, *Do the Right Thing* was not one of the five nominees for Best Pictures, nor was Lee among the candidates for Best Director. The film won only two nominations: Best Supporting Actor for Danny Aiello and Best Original Screenplay for Lee, the first African American to be nominated in that category. Lee was hurt by the oversights but wished to move on: "I'm just going to put it all behind me and show up [at the ceremony] and have a good time."

Lee found an outspoken ally at the Academy Awards ceremony. As actress Kim Basinger was about to introduce a clip from one of the Best Picture nominees, *Dead Poets Society* (which won the Original Screenplay award), she ignored the remarks prepared for her by the show's writers and made her

Spike Lee is shown arriving at the Academy Awards Ceremony in Los Angeles in March 1990. Although his film *Do the Right Thing* was nominated for Best Screenplay, there were some who thought it had been unfairly left out as a candidate for Best Picture.

own statement: "We've got five great films here. And they're great for one reason—they tell the truth. But there is one film missing from this list that deserves to be on it because, ironically, it might tell the biggest truth of all. And that's *Do the Right Thing*." An enthusiastic outburst of applause greeted her words. The television cameras zeroed in on a surprised and smiling Lee, who slipped Basinger a thank-you note after she returned to her seat.

Lee was not smiling when he visited Duke University in Durham, North Carolina, a few days later and discussed the reaction to his film with a group of students. "I think a lot of white Americans are more comfortable with a black man who's really a second-class citizen," he said, referring to the character portrayed by Morgan Freeman in *Driving Miss Daisy*, the Oscar winner for Best Picture. Lee argued that the film, which focuses on the relationship of a black chauffeur and his white employer, dealt with race relations in a way that was not threatening to whites: "Their comfort level is higher with [Morgan] driving around Miss Daisy than with Mookie throwing a garbage can through Sal's Pizzeria."

Nevertheless, Lee had much to be proud of. *Do the Right Thing* ranked as a major success, making up for the disappointing response to *School Daze* and restoring his status as an important filmmaker. It is also the film that has come to be considered Lee's masterpiece to date, ranking sixth in a poll of critics conducted by British film magazine *Sight and Sound*—an extraordinary achievement.

Besides its obvious qualities as a film, it also spurred a much-needed debate on racism and established Lee as a forceful advocate for racial justice who was not afraid to confront unpleasant truths. In his next film, with newly crowned Oscar winner Denzel Washington (Best Supporting Actor for *Glory*) as his star, Lee was once again preparing to tell a story that had never, in his view, been told before.

6

When a Man Loves Two Women

"I always knew I would do a movie about the music. When I say the music, I'm talking about jazz, the music I grew up with. Jazz isn't the only type of music I listen to, but it's the music I feel closest to."

Lee wrote these words in the companion book to his fourth feature film, 1990's *Mo' Better Blues*. For some, the idea of making a jazz film seemed to be a little tame, particularly considering the controversy and confusion caused by *Do the Right Thing*. Other skeptics, like Lee's studio, Universal, were far from convinced that *Mo' Better Blues* could fly: A pair of recent jazz films, Bertrand Tavernier's *'Round Midnight* (1986) and Clint Eastwood's *Bird* (1988), had been admired by film critics but fizzled at the box office.

For some, it seemed foolish for Lee to consider following up his most commercially successful film to date with something that could turn out to be an art-house film seen by only a limited audience. There was a reason behind Lee's decision, however: In his mind, *Mo' Better Blues* would make jazz—and, by extension, the African-American jazz musician—the centerpiece instead of a sidelight in a Hollywood motion picture.

Hollywood films had included some inspired musical performances by great black jazz and blues artists such as Bessie Smith (*St. Louis Blues*, 1929), Duke Ellington (*Black and Tan*, 1930), and Ethel Waters (*On with the Show*, 1931). Initially, however, only the stories of white jazz artists were deemed worthy of being told. The white man with a horn, juggling his professional and personal life, became the main dramatic formula for jazz-inspired films in the early 1940s. This genre hit its peak of popularity in the mid-1950s with *The Glenn Miller Story* and *The Benny Goodman Story*. When black artists were seen in these films, it was largely in cameo appearances as themselves; they performed their musical numbers and then quietly disappeared for the rest of the movie. At best, they might be cast as the white hero's wild right-hand man (Eddie "Rochester" Anderson to Bing Crosby in *The Birth of the Blues*, 1941) or teacher (Juano Hernández to Kirk Douglas in *Young Man with a Horn*, 1950).

Beginning in the late 1950s, films such as *St. Louis Blues* attempted to break new ground by featuring predominantly black casts, but the films tended to be short on plot and had little to say about the black culture that had actually produced jazz. In addition, they tried to mollify white audiences by introducing white characters who were paragons of virtue compared with the films' downtrodden black protagonists. Even the more recent *'Round Midnight* and *Bird*, despite the filmmakers' obvious respect for jazz, failed to truly analyze and fully capture the world of the black jazz artist. In those films, as well as in those that preceded them, the musician was not part of a black community with which the viewer could identify, his relationships with other blacks were often distant and

In *Mo' Better Blues*, Denzel Washington played Bleeck Gilliam, a fictional jazz trumpet player who faces professional and personal conflicts as he tries to make his way in the business. In particular, Bleeck is torn between two women, played by Cynda Williams (above, with Washington) and Joie Lee.

embattled, and the musicians were always troubled, unhappy, and overwhelmed with personal problems. Lee wanted to make a different kind of film, as he said, quoted in *Spike Lee: That's My Story and I'm Sticking to It*:

> It's like. . . . "Oh, these jazz musicians are so tormented, they never laughed, they never had joy in their life, they're all tragic and torn and twisted," Of course, that might have been a small part of it. But at the same time, I was thinking about the musicians I grew up with, of my generation. . . .

These guys weren't rich, but they were making good money. And they played basketball, football, they loved sports, they had family, they had girlfriends, had a good time going out, living—they're not simply moping around lamenting the misery of their lives.

In *Mo' Better Blues,* all of the ingredients for a successful jazz film, the good as well as the bad of the musicians' lives, come together. The main character, Bleek Gilliam (Denzel Washington), is a flawed man, but Lee shows *why* he is flawed. Bleek's name describes him perfectly: He is a somber gentleman, and because of his upbringing, he has invested his whole life, his whole being, in playing the trumpet. (In this, he is not unlike the usual film portrayal of a musician—but at least this time, he is a black musician!)

Bleek does have time, though, to juggle relationships with two women: Indigo (Joie Lee), a schoolteacher, and Clarke (Cynda Williams), an aspiring singer who wants a chance to perform with Bleek's group and to prove herself. Bleek, however, cannot see anyone's needs or talent but his own. He refuses to play music writen by the members who make up his group, the Bleek Quintet, and is constantly at odds with his saxophonist, Shadow Henderson (Wesley Snipes), over the direction in which the group is going and the amount of money they ought to be making. Shadow's interest (both professional and personal) in Clarke inevitably pushes the two men to a dramatic confrontation.

Bleek is also blinded by a sense of loyalty to his best friend and manager, Giant (played by Lee), whose lack of business savvy and gambling problems finally cost Bleek his career. While protecting Giant from a pair of hoods trying to collect a gambling debt, Bleek is bashed in the mouth with the one thing he loves: his trumpet. After the incident, he almost does what he once promised to do if he could not play his music: "roll up in a corner and die." He ends up settling down with

When Lee cast Denzel Washington in *Mo' Better Blues*, he was giving audiences a true black romantic lead for perhaps the first time ever. Though a few actors—like Sidney Poitier, shown above—had earned leading roles in Hollywood films, they were not given romantic storylines.

Indigo and having a child, while Clarke pursues a successful career, vocalizing with the Shadow Henderson Quartet.

The film has a distinct "jazzy" look, feel, and sound. Ernest Dickerson's cinematography accents Bleek's somber universe with plush hues of green, brown, and purple. Bill Lee's hot-house score samples different styles (from fusion to funk) but concentrates on classic jazz. Washington and the other principals did not really play their instruments in the film, but they fake it brilliantly, finally portraying in film the joy that a true musician has in exploring his art.

Besides attempting to accurately get the world of jazz onto the screen for the first time, Lee had other reasons for making his film. *Mo' Better Blues* would mark the first time since the mid 1970s that a major Hollywood film had a romantic black male lead. As we have seen, black actors were generally forced to play nonsexual, one-dimensional character "types." As with directors, however, black actors did occasionally manage to break through and land roles that went beyond stereotypes.

The great Paul Robeson, who spent most of his film career playing servants, finally got to show his talents in *The Emperor Jones*, the saga of a Pullman porter who becomes the dictator of a West Indian island, and Juano Hernández scored a triumph as a tough Southern farmer accused of murder in *Intruder in the Dust* (1949). During the 1950s, singer Harry Belafonte seemed capable of becoming a romantic matinee idol after making *Carmen Jones* (1954) and *Islands in the Sun* (1957), but his film career never really took off.

Even Sidney Poitier, a top box-office draw for many years and the first African American to win an Academy Award for Best Actor (*Lilies of the Field*, 1963), was usually obliged to play the "good Negro"—a professional man who was a model of good citizenship but devoid of any sexuality. (Since Poitier's victory, several other African-American actors and actresses have won the top prize at the Academy Awards, including Denzel Washington [*Training Day*, 2001], Halle Berry [*Monster's Ball*, 2001], Jamie Foxx [*Ray*, 2004], and Forest Whitaker [*The Last King of Scotland*, 2006]).

Even when Poitier's character had a love interest, he was not allowed to express his feelings in the same way that a white actor would. In 1967's *Guess Who's Coming to Dinner*, for example, the only act of affection between Poitier and his white fiancée is a casual kiss shown indirectly through a rearview mirror in a taxicab. Not until *For Love of Ivy* in 1968 was Poitier allowed to say "I love you" and follow it up with an uncompromising embrace and kiss. (In 1968, when white British pop singer Petula Clark touched Harry Belafonte on the arm during a television special, it caused headlines nationwide. It was the first time that a man and woman of different races had exchanged friendly body contact on American television.)

Lee's decision to cast Washington as Bleek was a milestone in giving audiences a true black romantic lead. Lee had seen Washington in a Broadway play in 1988. "The minute Denzel appeared on the stage, the women in the audience started screaming," Lee recalled. "Not only was Denzel a great actor, but he was a legitimate matinee idol. I wanted to write a role for him that black women were waiting for him to play. And, before I wrote one word of *Mo' Better Blues*, I knew I wanted [him] to play the lead."

Washington's intimate romantic scenes with Joie Lee and Cynda Williams were unlike any others previously filmed between black men and women. As Joie Lee explained, "In the scene where Bleek comes to visit Indigo after a gig, they're about to kiss and he descends on her like Count Dracula. When I saw [the filmed scene], it occurred to me that this was the first time I had seen such playful affection between a [black] couple on film."

Mo' Better Blues was a breakthrough film in one more aspect: the introduction of what would become Lee's "signature" shot, a way of filming a scene that Lee has used in most of his films. The shot is a dolly shot (a shot taken while the camera is in motion on a wheeled camera platform known as a dolly), described by Erich Leon Harris as "a shot that gives the effect of walking on a moving sidewalk." Lee further discussed the shot with Harris, saying, "The first time I used it was in

Mo' Better Blues with my character Giant. To get that shot you have to lay dolly tracks. Then you put the camera on the dolly. Then you put the actors on the dolly also. Then you move the dolly along."

All this filmmaking history was, for the most part, ignored by critics. Most of the reviewers praised Washington and Snipes, as well as Ernest Dickerson's moody cinematography, but some dismissed the story as being too choppy and contrived. (Richard Corliss of *Time* magazine flatly stated that with *Mo' Better Blues*, "Spike Lee gets mo' worse"). Once again, critics pointed out that his female characters seemed to exist only in relation to the male characters and not as people in their own right. They found it hard to believe that two smart, beautiful women like Indigo and Clarke would settle for a self-absorbed man like Bleek, even if he was played by Denzel Washington. Lee argued back at his critics, pointing out in *Essence* magazine that any portrayal he comes up with, regardless of whether it's a man or a woman is going to upset somebody. "I think my work, contrary to what some think, shows that I love women," he asserted. "I understand, though, where that type of criticism comes from. Black people have been so dogged out in the media, we're just—extra-sensitive. Many people are looking for Black Superwoman, Updated, with no faults. Uplifter of the race, strong, strong Harriet Tubman like. Do women like her exist? Yeah, but other types exist, too."

Lee was once again taken to task for not dealing with the subject of drugs, which have historically been part of the jazz scene. Lee dismissed that idea as racist but soon found himself being accused of being a racist himself. Some critics, as well as political commentators, found his portrayal of Moe and Josh Flatbush, the Jewish owners of the nightclub Beneath the Underdog (played by Italian-American actors John and Nicholas Turturro), to be anti-Semitic. "The brothers are caricatures, nothing but money-hungry Jews," one observer argued. "It's the kind of characterization that fuels anti-Semitism. I'm sure that if the roles were reversed, and they were black and made to look like blood-sucking buffoons, he [Lee] would be the first to say how degrading it is."

Lee countered that he was just showing the music world the way it is. "[Moe and Josh] don't represent all Jews," he said:

> They represent those Jewish agents, managers and club own-
> ers who have, over the years, ripped off black artists left, right
> and sideways. I remember all the stories my father and others
> would tell. That is a part of jazz music history, of all music
> history in this country, black people creating the music and
> white people reaping all the benefits. Many people just don't
> want to talk about, they don't want to acknowledge it at all,
> but I couldn't do the movie and ignore it.

Despite his explanations, the controversy grew to the point where Lee felt compelled to write an essay for the Op-Ed page of the *New York Times* under the heading, "I Am Not an Anti-Semite."

The negative publicity, mixed reviews, and traditional low turnout for films about jazz musicians may have hurt *Mo' Better Blues* at the box office. Made for $10 million, it earned back its budget but just missed the $20 million mark. All the same, many African Americans in the jazz world congratulated Lee for telling the story from their point of view and for analyzing the thorny issue of how an artist's dedication to his work can turn into a self-destructive obsession. As Donald Bogle observed, "*Mo' Better Blues* comes from a fresh perspective: that of a young African-American filmmaker who responds to jazz's rhythms, moods and textures—and who understands the place of the jazz hero."

There was a critical consensus that the film would have fared better if he had based it on the life of a real-life performer instead of a fictional one, but Lee felt that would have been a huge mistake. "Folks come to movies about real people with a lot of baggage, and if they don't see them the way they knew them or believed them to be, they will crucify you." That statement may seem to be a bit of an exaggeration (there have been plenty of successful "biopics" or biographical films about specific people), but it is true that the filmmaker does take a risk by making one. Everybody has his or her very different ideas about what Bill Clinton, for example, is like—some see him as a great president, others do not. A director risks alienating a large chunk of the movie-going audience by depicting the subject the way *he* sees him. Lee would take this risk of making a biographical film a few years later with *Malcolm X*, but not until he raised controversy by making a film about another "hot button" topic sure to stir up controversy and attention—sexual relations between a black man and a white woman.

7

Ebony and Ivory

On a humid Wednesday afternoon, August 23, 1989, Yusuf Hawkins, a 16-year-old African American from the East New York section of Brooklyn, joined a group of his friends on a trip to Bensonhurst, another area of the borough, to look at a used car they had seen advertised in a newspaper. Hawkins and his friends had no idea that they were venturing into a predominantly working-class Italian neighborhood on a day when racial passions were running particularly high. A young white woman in the area had argued with one of her friends and had told him he was going to be beaten up by her black boyfriend, who was coming to the neighborhood with some friends. The young man rounded up a group of his own friends, and, armed with sticks and a baseball bat, they waited for the black men to appear.

When Hawkins and his friends arrived in Bensonhurst, they found themselves confronted by a mob of angry white youths

In August 1989, 16-year-old Yusuf Hawkins, a black man from Brooklyn, went with his friends to look at a car for sale in the predominantly white neighborhood of Bensonhurst. Hawkins was killed when a scuffle erupted between Hawkins and his friends and a group of young white men from the area. In response, Reverend Al Sharpton led an anti-racism march through Bensonhurst, where the shooting took place.

ready and eager for a confrontation. They explained what they had come for, and the whites appeared to accept their story and began to relax. Just as the tensions began to subside, another white teenager appeared with a gun. Thinking that it was the group that he had been warned about, he began to fire wildly at the blacks, and one of the bullets struck Hawkins. By the time the paramedics arrived, Hawkins was lying dead on the sidewalk.

The city and the nation were stunned by the murder of Yusuf Hawkins. Black leaders and community activists, led by the Reverend Al Sharpton, staged a march through Benson-hurst to claim all New York City streets for all people, regardless of race. As if to underscore their point about the evils of racism, they were met by crowds of angry whites who shouted racial epithets and death threats at them. The harrowing scene, broadcast on national television newscasts, was reminiscent of the violent reaction to peaceful demonstrations in the South during the civil rights movement.

The political fallout was explosive. All four candidates vying for the office of mayor made an appearance at Hawkins's funeral; the incumbent, Ed Koch, running for an unprecedented fourth term for mayor, was booed by the attendees, many of whom were black. Koch also raised the ire of many African Americans and others in the city by criticizing any marches through Bensonhurst, arguing that they would only exacerbate the tension. Political pundits agreed that Hawkins's death mobilized the black vote in New York and motivated many whites to vote for Dinkins in the hope that New York's first African-American mayor could calm the racial conflicts in the city.

Lee was delighted with Dinkins's victory but was struck by one aspect of the Hawkins tragedy that no one was discussing. "Yusuf was killed because they thought he was the boyfriend of one of the girls in the neighborhood," argued Lee. "What it comes down to is that white males have problems with black men's sexuality. It's as plain and simple as that. They think we've got a hold on their women."

This insight, an extension of his exploration of romance and sexuality in *Mo' Better Blues,* served as the inspiration for *Jungle Fever.* Filmed entirely in New York, *Jungle Fever* tells the story of Flipper Purify (Wesley Snipes) and Angie Tucci (Annabella Sciorra). Flipper is an architect, and Angie is his new secretary. He lives in Harlem with his wife and daughter. She lives in Bensonhurst with her father and two brothers. While working late one night at the office, Flipper and Angie share small talk, Chinese food, and suggestive glances, and finally they begin a heated affair. They confide in their friends, who are not the least bit happy, particularly Flipper's buddy Cyrus (Lee). When Cyrus betrays Flipper's confidence in the name of "racial solidarity" and Angie's family also gets wind of what is going on, racism erupts on both sides of the divide, and both Flipper and Angie are driven from their homes.

Lee publicly stated many times that Flipper and Angie are supposedly drawn to each other because of the sexual myths about white women and black men (Flipper himself suggests this at the end of the film, when the lovers break up), but most critics agreed that this idea was not developed in the film. As Kathleen Carroll of the *New York Daily News* put it, "There's no hint of sexual heat in *Jungle Fever*, nor any emotional connection between Flipper and Angie. They cling together only after they are cast out of their homes."

Indeed, it sometimes seems in *Jungle Fever* that the interracial romance is really a device to bring audiences into a more complex urban world, where the ideas of black and white play themselves out in different ways every day. Flipper's professional and personal lives are in crisis. Facing racism at work, he is also forced to deal with the legitimate anger of his wife. Drew (Lonette McKee) not only feels deeply betrayed by her husband ("You had to eventually go get yourself a white girl, didn't you?") but also by a black society that has treated her coldly and cruelly because she is light skinned ("I told you how they called me high yellow, octaroon, quadroon, half-breed mongrel"), continuing the exploration of a theme begun in *School Daze.*

With her husband out of the house, Drew gets support from her African-American female friends during a humorously biting, spirited "war council." In a sort of roundtable debate, the women, who come in every hue of brown, talk about race and sex: white women who throw themselves at black men, black men who cannot handle "strong sisters," black women who scorn blue-collar black men in search of a "buppie" (black urban professional), and black men who want white women as "trophies." Considered the most hilarious—and brutally honest—scene in the film, the war council struck a very raw nerve in the African-American community.

Drew has her friends to turn to, but Flipper has no one to rely on for support. His father, the Good Reverend Doctor Purify (Ossie Davis), is a bitter man who also committed adultery and lost his congregation as a result. Despite this, he has no sympathy for Flipper's situation and chastises him for bringing Angie to his house for dinner. Flipper's mother, Lucinda (Ruby Dee), is a subservient woman who is always trying to keep the peace in her family but with little success.

Then there is Flipper's older brother, Gator (Samuel L. Jackson), who is addicted to crack cocaine. With his portrait of Gator, Lee finally silenced the critics who believed that his earlier films had sidestepped the drug problem. Here, he vividly documents the effects of the drug culture on those in it and outside it. In the film's most harrowing scene, Flipper searches the streets of Harlem for Gator, finding him in the Taj Mahal, "the Trump Tower of crack dens." Clearly Gator is a lost soul, beyond even the reach of his brother. This scene, set to Stevie Wonder's classic 1970s song "Living for the City," is one of the most powerful and nerve wracking that Lee has ever directed. From the beginning, Lee had a clear idea of how he wanted the scene to look, quoted in *Spike Lee: That's My Story and I'm Sticking To It*: "Ernest [Dickerson, his cinematographer] and I decided we wanted this to be like a living hell, Dante's Inferno.... We wanted to show, quite literally, our view of the devastation that crack has had and the souls that is taken. Ernest came up with this idea for the sound design. Every time you hear the pipes, there's this 'Whooosh' like their souls being sucked out of their bodies."

Despite the nightmarish images created by Lee, Jackson (who won a special supporting actor prize from the Cannes Film Festival) manages to put a human face on the character, portraying him as a sad and sardonic man whom the audience cannot help but pity. When Gator finally confronts his father, who has barred him from the house because of his drug use, the scene is genuinely heartbreaking.

Because of its unblinking treatment of class and color, *Jungle Fever* was hailed by many as Lee's best film. As Roger Ebert wrote in the *Chicago Sun-Times*, "It contains the fearless discussion of things both races would rather not face." *Newsweek* put Snipes and Sciorra on its cover and ran a question-and-answer feature with a half-dozen interracial couples, who were given tickets to the film and then asked their opinions of it. Lee himself was constantly asked if he had ever gone out with a white woman. "When I say no," he observed, "the press really has tried to turn it around like I'm saying that there are no attractive white women at all. It's just that people have their own preferences and my preference is black women. [Besides], I don't need the trouble. Like I don't have enough as it is!"

Lee never lacked critics, and some suggested that he had taken advantage of Yusuf Hawkins's death to attract audiences. In fact, *Jungle Fever* opens with a photo of Hawkins and a dedication to him. Later in the movie, a white character in Bensonhurst wears a T-shirt that says "Free Fama," referring to one of the youths accused of causing Hawkins's death. As *Jungle Fever* was playing in theaters, however, another highly publicized racial incident occurred in the New York area, proving that Lee was hardly overstating the problem. In this case, a popular black teenager on Long Island was almost clubbed to death with a baseball bat by a white schoolmate after being seen talking to a young white woman at a party. As Lee remarked in a television interview with Oprah Winfrey, "This stuff *still* happens. Race and sex have been intertwined in this country from the day we [Africans] were brought over on the boats, and I think the presence of Yusuf is throughout the whole film."

Jungle Fever scored well at the box office, earning more than twice its $14 million budget. Attention to the film was some-

In *Jungle Fever*, Flipper Purify (Wesley Snipes) and Angie Tucci (Annabella Sciorra) play an architect and a secretary who fall in love and begin an affair. They find themselves at odds with their families, who disapprove of their interracial romance.

what diluted by a spate of new films that Lee himself had made possible, however. Five years after Lee proved the viability of black films that spoke directly to the African-American experience, the powers that be in Hollywood finally understood that black audiences, which at the time accounted for nearly 25 percent of the movie-going public, represented a major market. In 1991, the studios released a dozen feature films directed by African Americans (all of them male). Films such as Joseph Vásquez's *Hangin' with the Homeboys*; Robert Townsend's *The Five Heartbeats* (the follow-up to his independent smash, *Hollywood Shuffle*); Mario Van Peebles's *New Jack City*; Bill Duke's *A Rage in Harlem*; Michael Schultz's *Livin' Large*; and Kevin

Hooks's *Strictly Business*, all showcased different elements of the black experience, and none would have been possible without Spike Lee's trailblazing efforts.

Other new young black filmmakers continued to emerge, inspired and influenced by Spike Lee. Nineteen-year-old Matty Rich went on local radio shows to raise the funds to produce and direct *Straight Out of Brooklyn*, an intense portrait of life in the Red Hook housing projects. John Singleton, then 23 years old and straight out of the University of Southern California's Film Writing Program, became an overnight sensation when he received a three-picture deal with Columbia based on his script for *Boyz n the Hood*, a deeply felt meditation on urban angst and violence in South Central Los Angeles. *Boyz n the Hood* became one of the highest-grossing movies ever directed by an African American, and, more important, it was cited on the Top 10 lists of many critics. Singleton became the first African American to be nominated for an Academy Award for Best Director.

The new black wave in filmmaking—often referred to as "New Jack Cinema"—was very different from the blaxploitation years. As cultural historian Henry Louis Gates Jr. observed, "Black filmmakers today are addressing social problems on the one hand, while addressing the depths of African-American culture on the other. They are taking the veil off of African-American cultural processes."

IN HIS OWN WORDS...

Discussing his film *Bamboozled* with Cynthia Fuchs, Lee said,

Violence is a part of America. I don't want to single out rap music. Let's be honest. America's the most violent country in the history of the world, that's just the way it is. We're all affected by it.

Black filmmakers, however, had to ask themselves whether Hollywood was really dedicated to supporting and sustaining the growth of black cinema or whether African-American films were just going to be another fad, like disaster films or breakdancing films. Like many of his peers, Lee was careful not to misinterpret the newfound interest of the establishment. He knew that doors open to black filmmakers in Hollywood could just as easily be slammed shut again if those same filmmakers did not use the opportunities given to them to work on improving their craft and find new ways to connect with their audiences.

Despite fears that the good times would not last; the sheer number of films, their realism, and the presence of so many blacks behind and in front of the camera were definite signs of progress. Lee saw it as an indication that the time was right for him to push forward to make what would be his biggest budget and perhaps most important film to date: the story of the man who had been a lifelong hero to Lee and several generations of African Americans: Malcolm X.

8

The Ultimate Test

This movie would be more than just a movie—it would be a political event. Although 27 years had passed since the assassination of Malcolm X, his legacy still inspired equal parts excitement and controversy. Some feared that a film that recreated his merciless attacks on American racism would fan the flames of racial antagonism; others believed that Malcolm X was a true American hero whose legacy should be honored as much as those of John F. Kennedy Jr. or Reverend Martin Luther King Jr. Spike Lee clearly belonged to the latter group, and his personal struggle to make *Malcolm X* was part of a much longer effort to bring the story of Malcolm X to the big screen.

The saga began in 1967, when producer Marvin Worth secured the rights to *The Autobiography of Malcolm X* for Warner Brothers Pictures. Skeptics both inside and outside Hollywood found the very concept of a Malcolm X film

Malcolm X, born Malcolm Little, became a hero to many Americans because of his efforts to end racism and segregation in America. Malcolm X is shown here waiting at a press conference in March 1964; less than a year later, he was shot and killed.

hard to digest. Why would Hollywood—an institution that Malcolm himself viewed as a bastion of white supremacy, a medium that for decades had unabashedly perpetuated the myth that blacks were inferior to whites—want to tell his story?

Although not obvious, the answer to that question was simple, as the autobiography detailed: Malcolm X was far more complex than most white people—and many blacks, for that matter—thought he was. There was more to him than the often-incendiary 30-second sound bites that he had given to the media on race relations during the height of his popularity in the late 1950s and early 1960s. Malcolm traveled a long road in his 39 years, and Worth wanted to capture the richness of his experience on film. It would prove more difficult than he had imagined.

The list of individuals who tackled the project in the 1960s, 1970s, and 1980s was impressive: novelists James Baldwin, David Bradley, and Calder Willingham; playwright David Mamet; and directors Sidney Lumet, Stuart Rosenberg, and Bob Fosse. Sooner or later, all of these accomplished men gave up, unable to come up with a vision that did Malcolm justice.

Finally, in 1990, Worth believed that he had struck gold when director Norman Jewison, playwright Charles Fuller, and actor Denzel Washington signed on. In 1983, all three men had worked together on the successful film adaptation of Fuller's Pulitzer Prize–winning drama, *A Soldier's Story*, one of several movies with racial themes for which Jewison had received wide acclaim. (The searing 1967 police drama *In the Heat of the Night*, which won the Academy Award for Best Film of 1967, was his most famous effort.) With such a talented and marketable trio involved, it seemed as if the film would finally be made.

Then Spike Lee, who had established himself as America's preeminent black filmmaker, heard about Jewison's involvement and began to campaign to get the directing job for himself. Instead of approaching Worth or Warner Brothers directly, he went straight to the media. "I have a big problem with Norman Jewison directing *The Autobiography of Malcolm X*," Lee told the *New York Times*. "That disturbs me deeply. It's wrong with a capital W. Blacks have to control these films.

Malcolm X is one of our most treasured heroes. To let a non-African-American do it is a travesty."

Lee's remarks set off a firestorm. Some, such as prominent playwright August Wilson, were quick to agree with him;

Malcolm X

A hero to generations of Americans, Malcolm X (born Malcolm Little in Omaha, Nebraska; May 19, 1925–February 21, 1965), was an African-American activist, American Black Muslim minister, and one-time spokesman for the Nation of Islam.

Malcolm X claimed that his father, a minister and follower of black nationalist Marcus Garvey, was murdered by racists in Lansing, Michigan, but some researchers believe that he actually died accidentally. When the family moved to Boston, Malcolm turned to a life of street crime and became known as "Detroit Red." In 1946, he was sentenced to 10 years in prison for burglary. Known in prison as "Satan" for his hatred of the Bible, God, and religion in general, Malcolm discovered the Black Muslims. He joined the group in 1952. He became a recruiter and changed his last name to "X"—meant to symbolize the rejection of "slave names" and the absence of a known African name to take its place. Malcolm received national attention through his writings (in which he referred to whites as "devils") and via a television documentary, both of which made him appear as an enemy of white people.

After breaking with the Nation of Islam in 1964, he founded the Muslim Mosque to bring the struggle for African-American rights worldwide and traveled to Muslim nations, where he was struck by their perceived lack of racial bias. Malcolm returned to the United States a changed man, convinced that whites were not inherently racist. He changed his name once again, this time to El-Hajj Malik El Shabazz, and founded the Organization of Afro-American Unity, through which he hoped to work with white organizations to further the cause of racial equality.

Only six months later, on February 21, 1965, Malcolm X was assassinated at the Audubon Ballroom in New York City. Three men, all members of the Nation of Islam, were convicted of his murder. That same year, *The Autobiography of Malcolm X: As Told to Alex Haley* was published, cementing Malcolm's reputation as a civil rights activist and thinker and "transforming the consciousness of a generation of African-Americans."

Wilson had previously stated that only an African American could direct the film version of his Pulitzer Prize–winning play *Fences*. Others accused Lee of "playing the race card," and this group included people once involved in the project.

"[This] is the story of a man who learns to transcend race," argued David Bradley. "[And] it's a stupid notion that there's a black aesthetic, a black experience. Malcolm never was a Christian—does that mean you have to have a Black Muslim director?" Sidney Lumet added, "I understand the black point of view. What does a white know? . . . . But where do you stop? Only an Irishman can direct Eugene O'Neill?"

Jewison was silent during the debate, more than likely because he and Fuller were agonizing over the material as well as over how to respond to Lee's statements. After it became clear that Fuller could not come up with a workable screenplay for the complicated subject, Jewison decided to bow out. "If I knew how to do it, I would move heaven and high water tomorrow to do it," he explained. "[Malcolm's] an enigma to me." He then added, "I know Spike wants to get involved and, at the moment, I would encourage him to because the film should be made." Thus the most expensive—and to some the most important—Hollywood movie with an African-American theme came to be entrusted to an African-American director.

The moment that Spike Lee and Warner Brothers inked the deal to direct *Malcolm X* was a milestone for African-American cinema. The film would mark the first time that an epic about blacks was directed by an African American and did not

IN HIS OWN WORDS...

If we become students of Malcolm X, we would not have young black men out there killing each other like they're killing each other now. Young black men would not be impregnating young black women at the rate going on now. We'd not have the drugs we have now, or the alcoholism.

feature a white actor as its star to ensure mainstream appeal. This stood in stark contrast to films such as the 1988 civil rights drama *Mississippi Burning*, which focused on the heroism of two fictitious white FBI agents while ignoring the role African Americans had played in the death of segregation, and *A Soldier's Story* (1983) and *The Color Purple* (1985), which, although centered on black heroes and heroines, had been entrusted to white directors.

Both Lee and his star, Denzel Washington, had an enormous amount riding on the hoped-for success of *Malcolm X*. Hollywood was watching to see whether Washington really had what it took to be a Hollywood leading man and still questioned whether Lee could become the first black director to successfully pilot a big-budget project. In addition, numerous interest groups were keeping a wary eye on the proceedings, convinced that only they knew how the story of Malcolm X could be filmed. Long before the movie actually opened in theaters on November 20, 1992, the off-screen drama promised to be nearly as intense as what would eventually end up on the screen.

As Lee began work on the script, based on the version written in 1969 by James Baldwin and Arnold Perl, he received a letter from a group called the United Front to Preserve the Legacy of Malcolm X. The members were concerned about how Lee would treat Malcolm's life on screen. They felt that, based on his previous films and the characters portrayed in them, Lee lacked the understanding necessary to portray the Malcolm X that they knew.

One of the founders of this group was noted writer and social critic Amiri Baraka, who had been inspired by Malcolm to adopt Islam. Baraka was a long-time critic who had also been upset by Lee's handling of a Muslim character in *Do the Right Thing*. As he told the *Washington Post*, "Am I not going to believe Malcolm X wouldn't be [like a] Radio Raheem, who was killed for playing his radio too loud? That is what racist

America would like to believe, that black [people] are killed because of something they did."

Baraka feared that Lee would sanitize and distort Malcolm's legacy to conform to traditional Hollywood storytelling conventions. "I do not want to see Malcolm's Detroit Red days [as a criminal and numbers runner] emphasized. I do not want to see the relationship with Elijah Muhammad [then the head of the Nation of Islam] de-emphasized. It was a critical and important influence and the film should show at what point they differed."

Baraka and his supporters staged a rally in Harlem, warning Lee not to "mess up Malcolm's life . . . so middle-class Negroes could sleep easier." Lee at first responded quite gently, saying on the black-owned station WLIB in New York, "I fully understand [their] concern on how Malcolm X will be portrayed. I have the same concerns they have." He later took a sharper tone when he talked to the *Amsterdam News*: "I'm gonna make the kind of film I want to make. And, who appointed Baraka chairman of the African-American arts committee? Nobody tells him what poems and plays to write, so why is he trying to tell me what kind of film to make? He can write whatever he wants, I want the freedom to make my films."

The issue, really, was whose Malcolm would be portrayed on the screen. With *Malcolm X*, Lee was facing the very thing that he had deliberately avoided with *Mo' Better Blues*: chronicling the life of a real person. Given the renewed interest in Malcolm X—"X" T-shirts and caps, produced by Lee's company, were being sported by teens throughout the country, and dozens of books and articles were being published about Malcolm and his philosophy; all of this due in no small part to the very fact that Lee was doing the film—it seemed obvious that there was a guaranteed audience for the film. With so many claiming Malcolm as their own, however—from Baraka to newly appointed Supreme Court Justice Clarence Thomas to a contingent of rap groups—producing a film that would satisfy all constituencies seemed impossible. (This was, of course, the very reason that Lee had avoided using the life of a real person for *Mo' Better Blues.*)

Lee would need the full cooperation of his studio to do the project as he envisioned it, but before filming had even begun, Lee and Warner Brothers were at odds over financing. Warner Brothers was willing to give him only $20 million and wanted a 2-hour, 20-minute film. The completed script—which ranged 30 years, called for thousands of extras, and included locations from Nebraska to South Africa—would result in a three and a half hours of film and would require a budget of at least $33 million. When Warner Brothers rejected this price tag, Lee protested that white directors were often tossed $40 million or more by the studios, no questions asked, and there was obviously a "glass ceiling" on how much they would spend on black films. (Warner Brothers had just spent close to $100 million on *Batman Returns.*) To justify its position, the studio made the point that the total U.S. gross of Lee's first five films was less than $100 million and that the highest budget he had ever worked with was $14 million for *Jungle Fever.*

Warner Brothers finally told Lee they would go as high as $28 million. Lee was still not satisfied, but, knowing that the studio would have a hard time pulling the plug on the project once shooting began, he signed. He then raised an additional $6.5 million by selling the foreign rights to the film and con- tributed $2 million of his $3 million directing fee directly to the film's budget. Lee declared, "I don't care what the budget is, I don't care what the contract says. Nothing's going to hurt the movie." Obviously, as in the days of shooting *She's Gotta Have It,* Lee was going to do whatever it took to make the movie that he wanted.

Initially, things went smoothly, and Lee and his crew were able to complete most of the major scenes during the first few months of shooting in Harlem and upstate New York. Then the cash crunch hit. When Lee began to run well over budget, the Completion Bond Company (CBC)—a group that ensures that a studio gets the picture it was promised within its proposed budget—thought that he should compromise when it came to the overseas locales. Why go to the Middle East when he could photograph Malcolm's pilgrimage to Mecca in Arizona or New Jersey? Why not just drop the South African sequence? Lee said no, and he got his way.

The CBC cut off payments in early spring 1992, when Lee had not delivered a rough cut of the film and it became obvious he had exceeded the agreed-on length of the picture. At this point, *Malcolm X* was $5 million over budget; the film did not yet have a score, it had not been edited, and postproduction work had just begun. When Lee realized that the CBC was working on replacing him and his editing staff, he set out to "do for self" (as Malcolm said). He secretly called on Bill Cosby, Oprah Winfrey, Prince, Janet Jackson, Magic Johnson, and Michael Jordan for help, and their contributions allowed Lee and his crew to keep working. "For two months, Warner and the bond company didn't know where the money was coming from," Lee recalled.

They, along with the rest of the world, found out when Lee broke the news on May 19, the sixty-seventh anniversary of Malcolm's birth. With actor Ossie Davis and Malcolm's widow, Dr. Betty Shabazz, by his side, Lee held a press conference. He revealed that he turned to celebrity heavyweights to keep his project going, thoroughly embarrassing the studio in the process. Indeed, the studio was caught totally off guard by the news but insisted that it had always planned to hand over more money and was only hoping to keep the overrun costs down. Two days after Lee's announcement, Warner Brothers reached an agreement with the bond company to settle the debts, and the film was completed.

When they finally saw the rough cut, Warner Brothers executives were alarmed by the film's opening title sequence. It begins with an American flag bursting into flames, its charred remains forming an *X*. At the same time, snippets of the 1991 beating of Rodney King by Los Angeles police officers are spliced in and Denzel Washington (as Malcolm) delivers a fiery speech about the crimes perpetrated against blacks by the white man in America and the rest of the world. Given the political climate concerning the American flag—Congress had just passed a law forbidding anyone to burn the flag in public—Warner Brothers got nervous. The studio did not ask Lee to change the opening, however, and he stated publicly that he would never have done so. "Anybody who sees it will [know] what it is saying," he remarked. "This ain't Walt Disney. This is about the present state of race relations in the world. I want to show that . . . almost all the stuff [Malcolm] talked about then, 30 years ago, is still happening today. And that, for the most part, nothing has changed. The injustices he talked about still have to be fought today."

The completion of the film did not mean that Lee was finished making waves. A full three months before *Malcolm X* was due to hit theaters, he began to pump the media mill. While addressing the convention of the National Association of Black Journalists in Detroit, he told the crowd to stay home from work and keep their children out of school on the day the film opened. If African Americans did not support the film, he asserted, Hollywood would have an excuse not to make another big-budget black-oriented film. Many educators and commentators blasted Lee for encouraging students to become truants, but he countered by saying that *Malcolm X* would provide the students with the "American history they are not getting in school. . . . They [can] go see the film and write a report."

Finally, after all the controversy and hype, *Malcolm X* had its opening in New York on November 18. Clocking in at 3 hours and 21 minutes, it is a true cinematic epic and, as film critic Roger Ebert said, "one of the great screen biographies." After Malcolm's early years in Omaha are explored through

Both Lee and the star of *Malcolm X*, Denzel Washington, had an enormous amount riding on the potential success of the film. Hollywood wanted to see if Washington had what it took to be a leading man and still questioned whether Lee could become the first black director to successfully pilot a big-budget project. Washington is shown here in a scene from the film that takes place in front of Harlem's famed Apollo Theater.

flashbacks, more than an hour of film time covers his life in the 1940s, when he was known as Detroit Red and operated as a street hustler in New York and Boston. During this period, while serving a prison term for robbery, Malcolm is introduced to the principles of the Nation of Islam and earns the nickname "Satan" for being proud of his African ancestry and challenging white ideals and authority. After his release from prison, Malcolm joins the Nation of Islam, and the group's leader, Elijah Muhammad (Al Freeman Jr.), replaces Malcolm's "slave" name, Little, with X, symbolizing the African family name Malcolm never knew.

The remainder of the film presents Malcolm's rise as a Muslim minister, his marriage to Betty Sanders (Angela Bassett), the effect of his incendiary rhetoric on white society, his break with the Nation of Islam, his pilgrimage to Mecca and the resulting softening of his beliefs, and his assassination. During the last 20 minutes, the powerful eulogy delivered by actor Ossie Davis at his funeral is heard as stills of the real Malcolm flash on the screen and anti-apartheid activist Nelson Mandela, on location in Soweto, South Africa, leads a class of students in a chant of "I am Malcolm," linking the struggle for the freedom of African people in America to those in the motherland.

Malcolm X is a lavish production that past masters of the Hollywood epic such as Cecil B. DeMille and David Lean would have been proud of. In it, Lee was able to fully use all that he had learned over the course of his career, proving himself to be, as Roger Ebert said, "one of the best filmmakers in America." The film was more than an exercise in great technical filmmaking, however; it was also a demonstration of how to make a film that both entertained and educated. Through Lee's direction and the performances of the entire cast, audiences learned the story of a self-made leader who experienced abject poverty, prejudice, and racism as a youth and prison as a young man. They learned of a civil rights leader who indicted whites, the "blue-eyed devils," for their oppression of black people and threatened retribution and vengeance for their crimes, but who came to adopt the view that whites could be good as well as bad and that all people are the same in the eyes of God. In the end, what *Malcolm X* reveals and celebrates is the evolution of a human being. As Lee stated, "We wanted to show that he was a person always in search of the truth, [that he possessed] humor, [was] very caring and warm, and constantly evolving."

Indeed, many were pleasantly surprised that Lee's film was so honest and even-handed, so approachable by black and white audiences alike. Roger Ebert commented on this, saying:

> I expected an angrier film than Spike Lee has made. This film
> is not an assault but an explanation, and it is not exclusion-
> ary. It deliberately addresses all races in its audience. White
> people, going into the film, may expect to meet a Malcolm X
> who will attack them, but they will find a Malcolm X whose
> experiences and motives make him understandable and
> finally heroic. . . . Reasonable viewers are likely to conclude
> that, having gone through similar experiences, they might
> also have arrived at the same place.

Other critics agreed. There was unanimous praise for Lee's
direction, as well as for Washington's performance, which
many considered his best to date. Mike Clark of *USA Today*
described *Malcolm X* as "an event movie that lives up to the
event." Reviewing the film for the *New York Times*, Vincent
Canby called Lee's epic "an ambitious, tough, seriously considered biographical film that, with honor, eludes easy characterization." Most critics were willing to bet that the film would
get serious recognition at Oscar time.

After a strong opening—on its first day, playing in 1,124
theaters throughout the nation, it took in $2.4 million—inter-
est in the film faded. Not even a clever half-price ticket offer
on January 18, the day the nation observed Martin Luther
King Jr.'s birthday, was able to entice moviegoers into theaters.
Moreover, Lee's hopes that *Malcolm X* would serve as a much-
needed history lesson for the hip-hop/MTV generation were
deflated when tracking polls done in urban centers such as
New York, Washington, D.C., Chicago, Miami, and Los Angeles showed that 15- to 24-year-olds made up barely a third of
the film's audience. It seemed that they may have wanted to
wear "X" T-shirts and hats but had little interest in seeing the
film and learning about the man himself.

By year's end, even the various awards groups seemed to
have lost interest in *Malcolm X* as well. Only the Chicago Film
Critics Association came through with a Best Picture cita-

tion, in addition to naming Washington Best Actor. The New York Film Critics Circle honored Washington but passed over the film. The following February, when the Academy Award nominations were announced, only Washington was on the list, along with costume designer Ruth E. Carter (neither won an Oscar). By the time *Malcolm X* finished its run in theaters, it had raked in $48 million. The figure represented a clear profit, but industry analysts had predicted double the amount, which made the film a disappointment in the eyes of Hollywood.

Some commentators claimed that Lee's ego and grandstanding had worked against the film, whereas others theorized that the nation had simply overdosed on "Malcolmmania." Lee himself expressed no disappointment. He insisted that the point of the film was neither to gross $100 million nor to win an Oscar. He believed he had accomplished something that no other black director in cinematic history had achieved, and he believed that he had every reason to be proud. Simply put, he had beaten the odds and produced a great film.

"When you do something this big and you have so many obstacles, either it can kill you or it makes you stronger," he explained. "And after going through the fire with this one, I feel I can do anything. [*Malcolm X*] was the hardest thing I've ever had to do in my life, and Denzel and the other filmmakers and the cast knew that . . . we had to make a great film."

And so he did—but then came the question "What would he do next?" He knew it wasn't going to be another epic. Lee needed to step back, retrench, and recharge his batteries. His next film would be a small, intimate picture, and, in its own way, as surprising a film as any he had previously made.

9

Spike Chills Out

"What do you do after *Malcolm X*?" That question began to buzz around Lee's head as soon as *Malcolm X* debuted on Thanksgiving weekend in 1992. Even if the film did not become a box-office bonanza or receive the accolades many believed were due, Lee had proved himself not only the leading black filmmaker of his generation but also one of the most versatile and dynamic directors of his time—black, white, or otherwise. Through the life of Malcolm X, he had captured the dreams, fears, and hopes of a nation. For a time, it was hardly possible to turn on a TV or radio, open a newspaper or magazine, or take part in a social event without being exposed to an intense debate about race, racism, race relations, American politics, black nationalism, or leadership in the African-American community. As *Malcolm X* made its way out of theaters during the spring of 1993, the public finally had a chance to catch its breath before his next movie hit the screen.

It was hard to imagine how Lee could follow up what many considered the most important motion picture made by a black filmmaker about a black subject—and the best Lee had ever done. Lee himself knew that, whatever that project was, it could not be another film of *Malcolm X*'s size and scope. "I didn't want to do two epics back-to-back," he explained. "I needed a chance to regroup. I really wanted to chill out a bit."

Lee's activities immediately after *Malcolm X* indicated that he was serious about his need for a breather. He almost disappeared from view after the 1992 Academy Awards, choosing not to grant any interviews—a stunning change of pace for a man who was usually willing to provide the media with a quote on just about anything. When he finally resurfaced that October, it was, surprisingly, at Riverside Church in Manhattan as a bridegroom. Lee had dated supermodel Veronica Webb for several years, but that fall he married Tonya Lewis, a Washington, D.C., attorney, in a ceremony attended by 300 guests. (Two years later, the Lees celebrated the birth of a daughter, named Satchel after the great baseball pitcher Satchel Paige.) In the weeks that followed, Lee started dressing the part of a married man: Instead of looking like a walking billboard for his movies, displaying his latest film-inspired jacket, cap, or T-shirt, he often appeared in slacks and sports jacket (unless he was off to a Knicks game at Madison Square Garden, in which case he usually wore his Knicks regalia). When Lee then revealed that his seventh film would be *Crooklyn*, a "dramedy" about a two-parent black family in Brooklyn during the early 1970s, there seemed to be little doubt that the one-time renegade had mellowed.

Lee conceded that marriage had indeed affected him. He contended, however, that the perceived change from single, young, angry black male to humble, hospitable family man had more to do with image than reality. "I know who Spike Lee the filmmaker is and I also know who Spike Lee the person is, and while they are one and the same they are two totally different people," he explained. Because of his reputation for being confrontational and controversial, Lee said, "people tend to believe that I am wired up and ready to attack at all times. I can get fired up, no question. But nobody can be on automatic 24-7, 365. And I am not as serious as some might want to believe. There are sides to me that people don't know about, and much of that comes out in the work I do."

Crooklyn was Lee's opportunity to show another side of himself. This film was nonconfrontational, noncontroversial, and nonpolitical—and a definite departure from his previous work. His earlier films had concentrated on conflict between adults on racial, sexual, social, cultural, economic, and political grounds. *Crooklyn*'s protagonist is a 10-year-old girl, Troy Carmichael (Zelda Harris). Troy has grown up as a tomboy and is just beginning to discover and assert herself as a female. She also struggles to find space in a house where she is the middle child and the only girl out of five children, forcing her to learn how to stick up for herself when she is pushed aside or pushed around.

Troy is able to cope with the growing pains because of the close relationship she has with her mother, Carolyn (Alfre Woodard). Strict and stern, Carolyn tolerates no nonsense from her children—or her husband, Woody (Delroy Lindo), a musician whose stubborn dedication to his art prevents him from bringing home a steady paycheck. When Troy returns, a little older and wiser, from visiting relatives in the South, she learns that her mother is dying of cancer. She then has to cope with the prospect of entering her teenage years as the woman of the household, without her mother's guidance.

The plot bears a rather striking resemblance to the story of Bill and Jacquelyn Lee and their children. In the film credits, Spike, Joie, and Cinque Lee are listed as co-screenwriters. In fact, Joie came up with the idea to do *Crooklyn*, and she and Cinque collaborated on a script, developing it first as a television series. Those plans did not work out, but, believing that

Lee poses with his family prior to a film screening. He is shown here with his wife, Tonya Lewis, his daughter Satchel, and his son Jackson Lewis. After his wedding in 1992, Lee admitted that marriage had softened him a bit.

the story was still a good one, Joie and Cinque refashioned their material into a film script. When they finished the first draft, they showed it to Spike, who loved it. "It was all over the place," he recalled, "but it was *there*. I said, 'OK, let me put my spin on it.'"

Despite the clear family connection, Lee insisted that "I never saw this film . . . as a film about my family. There were certain things that resembled our family, and that, in fact, are our family. But it is very, very loosely based on [our] recollections growing up. We always saw it as a film, not the story of the Lee family." Those close to the family, though, insisted that Lee wanted to discourage the comparison because he and his siblings were concerned about the reaction of their father, Bill.

Relations between Spike and his father had seen their ups and downs over the years. Shortly after Jacquelyn Lee's death, Bill Lee had become involved with and soon married Susan Kaplan, a white Jewish woman who Spike Lee blamed for destroying their family. Although Bill Lee did compose the score for Lee's student films and his first three feature films, he was replaced on *Mo' Better Blues* by Terence Blanchard. The change was undoubtedly an additional source of family tension. Finally, in the midst of Lee's backbreaking efforts at filming *Malcolm X*, he learned that his father had been arrested for heroin possession. Since then, the two spoke to one another only on occasion—"depending on the weather," in Lee's words. Any feeling on Bill Lee's part that he had been portrayed in a bad light could only create more tension between him and his son.

A DIFFERENT WORLD

Crooklyn dramatizes a world that some would probably find hard to believe ever existed. The one square block on which the film takes place is lined with well-kept brownstones. In the summer weather, the children play games on the sidewalk and in the street. The closest thing to a menacing presence in the community is a couple of glue sniffers (one of them played by Lee) who get high inhaling the fumes of Elmer's, but they are more scared of themselves than others are of them.

Crooklyn recaptures a time of tranquility and innocence that Lee remembered well and wished was still the rule in black communities. "We were able to have childhoods," he explained.

> The worst thing that could happen to us was some kid would bloody your nose comin' home from school. We had water guns, G.I. Joe Bazookas. You know, toy guns. Kids got guns nowadays. And kids were not exposed to drugs. Not to say that there wasn't heroin or pot, but kids were not exposed to it. I never had to worry about getting into fights, or think, "Am I going to get hit by that errant bullet?"

Lee had no doubt why things changed for the worse:

> I think it was because of [President Ronald] Reagan cutting the federal programs and tinkering with the Supreme Court, and trying to take back a whole lot of civil rights stuff that people had fought and died for over the years. Because of that, the combination of drugs and crack is really devastating generations upon generations. There's been a deterioration not just in Brooklyn, but in all the U.S.A.—all of urban America. The violence now follows you no matter where you go—it's not just in the inner-city, it's even in the suburbs.

For these reasons, Lee felt that *Crooklyn* had to be done:

> I wanted to show that, despite what White America thinks, there's at least *one* family—one family in [a] Hollywood [film] this year, anyway—where both parents are *there*, where the mother's not on crack, walkin' the corner, where the family's not on welfare, the sons aren't rapists and muggers, and the daughters aren't out getting pregnant at the age of eight. [The Carmichaels] are a normal family who fight and fuss and love. But they're not dysfunctional.

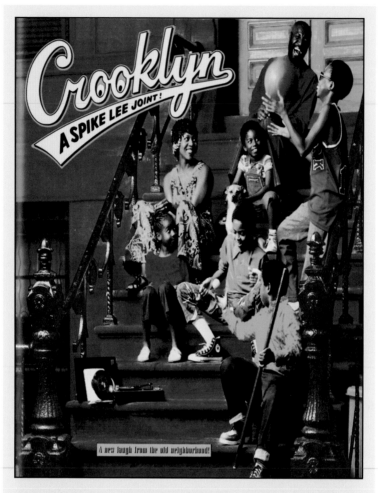

After the intensity and drama of making *Malcolm X*, Spike Lee wanted to make an entirely different movie. That is how the concept for *Crooklyn* came about; he wanted to portray a normal family and the struggles they undergo in a small neighborhood in Brooklyn. Above is the cover of the DVD edition of the film.

Like all of Lee's films, *Crooklyn* has a distinct black flavor. The fashion and hair of the day are brought back in full effect, and the experience of picking an afro and being forced to eat black-eyed peas are recalled in hilarious snapshots of black life.

All of the action plays out against two dozen soul classics by artists like the Staple Singers, Aretha Franklin, the Jackson 5, Stevie Wonder, and the Stylistics, all of which helped to bring the era back to life.

Crooklyn opened to generally warm reviews. Gene Siskel and Roger Ebert gave it "two thumbs up" and dubbed it "a funny, loving [family] portrait." Joel Siegel of ABC's *Good Morning America* said it was "very funny" and added, "It's the movie to see." Despite the critical praise, *Crooklyn* did poorly at the box office, barely making back its $15 million budget. Lee had been afraid that the film would not find an audience, especially coming on the heels of a project like *Malcolm X*. "People might have been looking for something a little more emotionally hyped," he reflected. "There are those who expect something when they come to a Spike Lee Joint, and I guess they didn't see that with *Crooklyn*."

Spike's next film, *Clockers*, would be the first that had not begun life as a "Spike Lee Joint" (what Lee calls all of his films) or, like, *Malcolm X*, as a project that he had wanted to make for years. *Clockers*, based on the bestselling novel by Richard Price, was originally slated to be directed by fellow NYU Film School graduate Martin Scorsese and to star Robert De Niro. Things changed, though, as Lee recalled in *Spike Lee: That's My Story and I'm Sticking to It*: "Martin Scorsese said he had been working on *Clockers* with Richard Price but decided to do *Casino* instead. He said he wanted me to direct it and for him to produce. So I read the script and I read the novel, and I liked the novel very much."

Although he liked the novel, he was not sure that the project was for him. "At first I didn't want to do it," Lee said. "These hip-hop, gangsta, shoot-'em-up films have been done to *death*. But, then I thought, maybe this can end it all." Lee planned to do something that, in his eyes, many of the "hood" films about inner-city life (those released after *New Jack City* and *Boyz n the Hood*) failed to do. "Folks just don't fall into a life of drugs and crime because they are inherently bad. I thought I could show that a so-called thug has a conscience, that he is a person."

Price was happy about that. "When white people view a film, they view blacks as Other with a capital O," he said. "But Lee breaks down the wall of otherness in his films, and I've never seen it done so matter-of-factly [as it is in *Crooklyn*]. You sit there and realize these people on the screen are just like your family, your friends. They are human beings, too—and *that* is the power of filmmaking."

For Lee to make the movie he wanted to make, though, there would have to be change to the screenplay. The novel tells the story of a policeman, Rocco Klein, trying to bring down a low-level drug dealer, a "clocker" named Strike. With Robert De Niro starring in the film, the emphasis would have been placed on Klein, the policeman. With Lee directing and cowriting the screenplay, the emphasis was shifted to Strike, who heads a team of drug dealers who work on a corner of the Nelson Mandela Projects in New York City.

Lee's long-time film editor, Sam Pollard, was not surprised by the change of emphasis:

> Spike being the director that he is, he didn't just take Richard Price's script and shoot it. He reworked it. Spike turned it around and made it from the point of view of Strike, which really makes the film fascinating if you think about films from an anthropological perspective. This is a very powerful film about the African-American experience in the inner city and how young men struggle to negotiate life.

In other words, Lee took Price's material and made it his own, turning the film into a true Spike Lee Joint.

Filmed with the hyper-real quality of a stylized documentary, *Clockers* follows the cat and mouse battle between the white policeman and Strike, who, the policeman is convinced, has murdered another dealer in a fast-food restaurant. Lee uses this basic murder mystery framework as a means to explore the plague of guns and black-on-black crime that are destroying America's inner cities. The movie takes the viewer into a world that he or she often sees only briefly on the evening news, and, although not offering any easy solutions, it presents a world in which the options for young people seem to include little more than a career in drug dealing followed by an early death.

The film, which contained some of Lee's most assured work to date, received mixed reviews and did poorly at the box office, with a domestic gross of just $13 million against a cost of $25 million. (The film eventually made its costs back from international sales and video rentals.) The majority of the unfavorable reviews came from fans of Price's book, who were annoyed and angered that Lee had told only half of the story. Lee was convinced that the film failed at the box office because it was a story without heroes, a story that told the truth about that kind of life. Editor Sam Pollard agreed, saying, "*Clockers* didn't make any money because, in my opinion, it's a true depiction of what is going on the 'hood. . . . If you watch *New Jack City* or *Menace II Society*, all those films have a little glamour. This one doesn't. It *was* the nail in the coffin. But people didn't get it. They're starting to get it now."

A STRING OF BOX OFFICE DISAPPOINTMENTS

Clockers was a box office disappointment, and Lee's next film, *Girl 6*, fared even worse. This film, which explored the life of a struggling actress trying to make ends meet by working for a phone sex line, earned less than $5 million against a cost of $12 million. Even worse, from Lee's point of view, the film earned some of the most negative reviews of his career. Critics were unable to understand what the film was trying to do and complained about the one-dimensional characters and somewhat unbelievable motivations.

Even Roger Ebert, one of Lee's strongest defenders, had harsh words to say about the film, once again pointing out Lee's weakness in writing about and understanding his female characters (a definite drawback in a film featuring a female protagonist): "Spike Lee is a great director, but his strong point is not leading expeditions into the secret corners of the female psyche. . . . *Girl 6* is Spike Lee's least successful film, and the problem is two-fold: He doesn't really know and understand [the character] Girl 6, and he has no clear idea of the film's structure and purpose."

Lee's next film, *Get on the Bus* was considered by many critics as a return to form. Released in 1996, it follows a group of about 20 black men taking a cross-country bus trip to join the Million Man March. Intriguingly, rather than using studio financing, Lee approached prominent African Americans to invest in the film—"black seed-investment for a black business," as he called it. Made for just $2.5 million and shot inexpensively on 16-mm

Million Man March

The Million Man March was a march by African-American men organized by Nation of Islam leader Louis Farrakhan in Washington, D.C., on October 16, 1995. The event included efforts to register African Americans to vote in U.S. elections and to increase black involvement as volunteers and working in their home communities.

Many whites had mixed feelings about the event, largely because of some of the controversial figures involved with it (such as Louis Farrakhan himself, long criticized as racist, sexist, and anti-Semitic). Indeed, many criticized the march itself as being sexist because it was a male-only event.

The turnout for the event did not quite reaching the "million man" level, but it was still extraordinarily high, with a final estimate of more than 800,000 marchers. The results of the march went beyond that day, however. In the months after the march, 1.5 million black men registered to vote, as the idea of black power and unity continued to spread and have a positive impact throughout the country.

film and video, the movie was in many ways a throwback to his early days as a filmmaker: shot quickly and on the cheap.

Get on the Bus is a movie of conversation and illumination: As Lee said in an interview with Erich Leon Harris in *Moviemaker*, "We wanted everybody to have their say on this bus, because in a lot of ways each person has to stand for some ideology or some aspect of African-American men." With a cross section of African-American men as characters, Lee was able to examine racism, attitudes toward blacks and whites, and unity and division within the black community, all within a two-hour, highly entertaining film.

As usual, Roger Ebert was Lee's most understanding critic:

> What makes "Get on the Bus" extraordinary is the truth and feeling that go into its episodes. Spike Lee and his actors face one hard truth after another, in scenes of great power. I have always felt that Lee exhibits a particular quality of fairness in his films. "Do the Right Thing," was so even-handed that it was possible for a black viewer to empathize with Sal, the pizzeria owner, and a white viewer to empathize with Mookie, the black kid who starts the riot that burns down Sal's Pizzeria. Lee doesn't have heroes and villains. He shows something bad—racism—that in countless ways clouds all of our thinking. "Get on the Bus" is fair in the same sense. . . . This is a film with a full message for the heart, and the mind.

REALITY TELEVISION

Few major directors in Hollywood could equal Lee's achievement of making 10 feature films in his first 10 years as a director. Not all the films achieved critical or popular success, but they were all obviously the work of a gifted filmmaker—one who remained determined to make the movies that he wanted to make and to make them his way. As if to prove wrong the critics who thought he was making too many movies, Lee added television to his list of accomplishments—and received some of his best reviews to date. The film, called *4 Little Girls*, was his first documentary. It told the story of one of the most shocking days of the American civil rights struggle.

It happened on September 15, 1963, in Birmingham, Alabama, at the three-story 16th Street Baptist Church, a longtime rallying point for civil rights activities. On that early Sunday morning, during the church's Youth Day, three United Klans of America members planted 19 sticks of dynamite in the basement of the church. At about 10:25 A.M., when 26 children were walking into the basement assembly room for closing prayers, the bombs exploded. Four girls—Addie Mae Collins (age 14), Denise McNair (11), Carole Robertson (14), and Cynthia Wesley (14)—were killed in the blast, and 22 more children were injured.

This brutal, racially motivated terrorist incident was intended to instill fear in those who supported equal civil rights. Instead, it caused public outrage throughout the country and galvanized the civil rights movement to further success. The tragedy was a major turning-point in the civil rights movement.

Lee had wanted to make a documentary about the attack since he had graduated from NYU Film School. Although nothing came of it then, he always kept the idea in the back of his mind. He was inspired to take on the topic after a spate of church bombings in the mid-1990s. "I've always wanted to do a full feature length documentary and this subject matter was just calling out to be done," Lee said in an interview with actor Delroy Lindo in 1999. He continued,

> I wanted to go back and try to bring to life these four girls, who they were, and also what they might've become, by talking to their parents and relatives, and put it within the context of that pivotal moment in American history, you

know, the Civil Rights movement, and Birmingham was the focal point. I wanted the people who were there, who were right up in it. No one could tell us better than the people who were there.

HBO agreed that the time was right to make the film and gave Lee the funding he needed. The cable network was so pleased with the end result that, in addition to showing the movie on television, they also screened it at a movie house in New York City, making it eligible for the Academy Awards in the category of Documentary Feature. The movie received nearly unanimous rave reviews, along with an Oscar nomination. On award night, March 23, 1998, *4 Little Girls* was considered the favorite to win. It lost to *The Long Walk Home*, which told of the struggle for Jewish Holocaust survivors to survive in the years immediately after World War II. Although disappointed at the loss, Lee was not entirely surprised: On the DVD for *4 Little Girls*, he said, "If there's one thing you can bet the bank on, if there is a Holocaust film in the Academy Awards you are not going to win."

KEEPING BUSY AND GETTING GAME

Spike Lee is not a man who likes to take it easy. In the same year that he made *4 Little Girls*, he also formed Spike DDB, an advertising agency aimed at the urban/hip-hop market; directed music videos for Bruce Hornsby, Chaka Khan, and Curtis Mayfield; celebrated the birth of his son, Jackson; and taught film at NYU. In addition, he indulged in his favorite pastime—cheering on his favorite sports team, the New York Knicks.

For years, Spike Lee has been a permanent fixture at Knicks games at Madison Square Garden in New York, where his courtside rooting sometimes attracts as much attention as the action on the floor. In June 1994, for example, when the Knicks were engaged in a heated playoff contest with the Indi-

Spike Lee is a huge fan of the New York Knicks basketball team. He is often spotted watching the game courtside; he has even been known to participate in the game by heckling players on the opposing team. He is shown here at the 1994 playoff game between the Knicks and the Chicago Bulls.

ana Pacers, Lee nearly became a participant: He spent much of the game taunting Pacers star Reggie Miller, hoping to throw him off his game. Unfortunately for the Knicks, Miller eventually went on a scoring spree that won the game for the Pacers. Miller sank shot after shot, repeatedly gesturing toward Lee and returning the filmmaker's abuse. After the game, a number of fans and sportswriters blasted Lee, blaming him for inspiring Miller and contributing to the Knicks' defeat. Much to Lee's relief, the Knicks came back to win the series. "It would've been a very long summer [otherwise]," he admitted when interviewed at the Garden the following season.

Lee's defenders, such as *New York Times* basketball writer Harvey Araton, have pointed out that Lee has been faithfully attending Knicks games since he was a teenager, always paying for his own tickets even when he could afford only the cheap seats up in the rafters. He also attends every Knicks playoff game at the Garden, even flying home in the middle of the Cannes Film Festival in order to root for his team. "It's the drama, the tension," Lee said, explaining his enthusiasm to Araton. "I mean, you come to the game, you don't have lines. You can't write this material. There's always the chance you'll see something great." Indeed, Lee is such a huge basketball fan that, in 1998, he wrote a book on the subject. Called *The Best Seat in the House: A Basketball Memoir*, the book chronicles his lifelong love affair with the game.

Lee also released his twelfth film in 1998. *He Got Game*, starring Denzel Washington, looks at basketball from a different angle. Denzel Washington plays Jake Shuttleworth, a convicted felon doing time for killing his wife. His son, played by Ray Allen, is a highly talented basketball player being recruited by some of the top college basketball programs in the country. Jake is temporarily released from prison by the governor in the hope that he can persuade his son to sign with the governor's college. If he does so, the governor will reduce his sentence. From this rather far-fetched scenario, Lee made a film that looked deeply into the world of college basketball recruiting and the promises that are made to inner city athletes, the dynamics of the father-son relationship, the effects on young black men of growing up with absent fathers or parents, and the question of how to choose between material gain and the "right thing" to do.

The movie opened to generally strong reviews, with critics like Roger Ebert calling it Lee's best film since *Malcolm X*. The magazine *Time Out London*, though, ended its relatively positive review by saying that "most scenes play too long, with a surplus of ideas, textures, tones and characters, and after 134 minutes it's clear Lee's problem with closure hasn't gone away."

Without exception, however, the critics agreed on one point: The soundtrack to *He Got Game* was one of the finest for any Spike Lee film. By juxtaposing the music of American classical music composer Aaron Copland with that of Public Enemy, Lee broke new musical ground. "Spike uses music in very unexpected ways," said music supervisor Alex Steyermark in *Spike Lee: That's My Story and I'm Sticking to It*. He continued,

> It is really bold: if I have to pick a quality that I've learned from Spike, it is that I've learned to be bold. Go for it, visually, stylistically, musically. He likes bringing together different cultural elements in music. And only Spike would bring together Aaron Copland and Public Enemy. But they are both quintessentially American music icons: Copland from Brooklyn, the quintessential American classical composer, and Public Enemy are the equivalent to hip-hop.

BACK TO THE SUMMER OF '77

Inspiration for films can come from unexpected places. At the premiere of *Girl 6*, actor/writer Michael Imperioli (best known for playing Christopher Moltisanti on *The Sopranos*), who had acted in *Jungle Fever, Malcolm X, Clockers*, and *Girl 6*, presented Lee with a screenplay he had written with a partner, Victor Colicchio. It was called *Anarchy in the Bronx*. Lee's initial impulse was to tell Imperioli that he should direct it and that Lee would executive produce it. After failing to find a studio to finance a film directed by first-time director Imperioli, Lee announced that he would direct it himself.

The decision made perfect sense. The screenplay, now entitled *Summer of Sam*, takes place in New York City, largely in the Bronx, during the summer of 1977—the year that Lee decided to become a filmmaker and the year he directed *Last Hustle in Brooklyn*. It was, in a way, a return to his roots as a filmmaker.

Lee described his reasons for making the film in a 1999 interview with Stephen Pizzello, published in *Spike Lee Interviews*:

> I grew up in New York, and I found that whole summer to be significant. What I really want to try to emphasize to people about this film is that it is not just about the Son of Sam—David Berkowitz. This film is about how the Son of Sam killings affected and changed the lives of eight million New Yorkers during that particular summer.

That summer was also one of the hottest summers on record; the summer when disco was at its peak and Studio 54 had just opened; the summer of the beginnings of punk music; and the summer that Reggie Jackson joined the Yankees. *Summer of Sam* captures it all, bringing to life a city in transition, a city in crisis.

Once again, Roger Ebert expressed his deep understanding of Lee's work, pointing out that

> "Spike Lee's *Summer of Sam* is his first film with no major African-American characters, but it has a theme familiar to blacks and other minorities: scapegoating. In the summer of 1977, when New York City is gripped by paranoid fear of the serial killer who called himself the Son of Sam, the residents of an Italian-American neighborhood in the Bronx are looking for a suspect. Anyone who stands out from the crowd is a candidate.
>
> Lee's best films thrum with a wound-up energy, and *Summer of Sam* vibrates with fear, guilt and lust. It's not about the killer but about his victims—not those he murdered, but those whose overheated imagination bloomed into a lynch mob mentality. . . . *Summer of Sam* is like a companion piece to Lee's *Do the Right Thing*. In a different neighborhood, in a different summer, the same process takes place: the neighborhood feels threatened and needs to project its fear on an outsider.

BLACKS AND THE MEDIA

If *Summer of Sam* was a harrowing look at a city in fear, Lee's next film was nothing but entertainment. It was a concert film, a film document of the highly successful show entitled *The Original Kings of Comedy*, which showcased four black stand-up comics: D.L. Hughley, Cedric the Entertainer, Steve Harvey, and Bernie Mac. The tour had been a smash hit with black audiences, and the movie followed suit. It became a somewhat unexpected box office hit and earned nearly $40 million.

The film's box office success came too late to be used as a bargaining tool as Lee negotiated to make his next film, *Bamboozled*. As producer John Pierson noted in *Spike Lee: That's My Story and I'm Sticking to It*, "Spike is the guy who in commercial terms has really never had a breakout hit, unless you count *The Original Kings of Comedy*. It is difficult when somebody is deciding what they can afford to give you as a budget, based on what you have returned in your last three or four films. It doesn't matter what you have done over your whole career."

It must be a source of constant frustration to Lee to continually have to "sell" himself to Hollywood, to constantly have to convince Hollywood moneymen that his next project is a worthwhile investment. In *Bamboozled*, Lee created a film that expressed his discontent with Hollywood and its treatment and portrayal of African Americans.

BAMBOOZLED

In *That's My Story and I'm Sticking to It*, Lee wrote:

> Its origin is really in one of my first films at NYU, *The Answer*, in which a young African-American screenwriter is asked to write and direct a $50 million remake of *Birth of a Nation*. This guy sells his soul to the devil to do that film. And we intercut the film with some of the worst racist

scenes from the so-called greatest film ever made. *Bamboozled* revisits that, because if you look at that character in *The Answer* and at Pierre Delacroix in *Bamboozled,* there are various similarities.

If *Summer of Sam* was Lee's expansion of his student film *Last Hustle in Brooklyn, Bamboozled* was his expansion of *The Answer,* his satirical look at the ways in which blacks are portrayed in the media. In satire, the artist uses humor, exaggeration, and ridicule to point out human or societal vices. Although satire is usually meant to be funny, its purpose is not necessarily the humor itself but the artist's use of humor to express disapproval of the artist's subject. *Bamboozled,* though, confused its audiences, who did not quite know how to interpret the movie's somewhat uneasy mix of humor and drama or how to take the movie's reimagining of the minstrel show.

The minstrel show was a form of popular American entertainment made up of comic skits, variety acts, dancing, and music performed by white people in blackface, or, in the years after the American Civil War, by African Americans in blackface. Minstrel shows portrayed blacks in stereotypical and insulting ways—as ignorant, lazy, superstitious, joyous, and musical. These shows, which faded in popularity only by the mid-twentieth century, played a large role in creating a negative image of blacks in the minds of white America.

Bamboozled played on that historical fact by showing an African-American television producer who, criticized for not being "black enough," creates a new show, "Mantan: The New Millennium Minstrel Show." It stars two homeless black street performers wearing blackface, is set in a watermelon patch on a plantation, and includes every ugly stereotype of black behavior ever used in the minstrel shows of days passed. As described in the *New York Times* review of the movie, "Mantan" was a huge hit and was "embraced . . . by a multiracial audience, who accept the show as a hip, ironic celebration of black culture laughing at itself."

For many critics of the film, the very act of the black actors wearing blackface, traditionally worn to emphasize stereotypical "black" features was a step too far. Even Roger Ebert, normally one of Lee's most sympathetic critics said:

> The film is a satirical attack on the way TV uses and misuses African-American images, but many viewers will leave the theatre thinking Lee has misused them himself.
>
> That's the danger with satire: To ridicule something, you have to show it, and if what you're attacking is a potent enough image, the image retains its negative power no matter what you want to say about it. *Bamboozled* shows black actors in boldly exaggerated blackface. . . . Can we see beyond the blackface to its purpose? I had a struggle.

Many people found the whole topic too difficult and controversial to take; some, such as Andrew O'Hehir at Salon.com called the film "a near masterpiece ambiguously balanced between brilliance and incoherence," but audiences stayed away from the movie.

Lee may have been taken aback at the film's failure at the box office. Although the film was not entirely successful, it was certainly one of his most daring and challenging films, asking questions that nobody else would dare to bring up in films. Are whites so challenged by blacks on television that they will only watch them when they are funny and thereby nonthreatening? Are gangsta-rap videos the modern-day equivalent of the minstrel shows, portraying demeaning and negative black images for the enjoyment of a largely white audience? Are whites who embrace hip-hop and try to "act black" wearing a new form of blackface? As Stephen Holden said in *The New York Times*, "*Bamboozled* is . . . an important Hollywood movie. Its shelf life may not be long, nor will it probably be a big hit, since the laughter it provokes is the kind the makes you squirm. But that's what good satire is supposed to do. Out of discomfort can come insight."

BOX OFFICE DISAPPOINTMENTS

Few expected huge audiences for *Bamboozled*, but Lee's next film, *25th Hour*, was a definite disappointment. The film, which starred Edward Norton, Philip Seymour Hoffman, and Rosario Dawson, told the story of a convicted drug dealer's last day of freedom before starting a seven-year prison sentence and was Lee's first film to be set in a post 9/11 New York City. The reviews ranged from so-so to excellent. In the *San Francisco Chronicle*, Mick LaSalle called it "a film of sadness and power, the first great twenty-first-century movie about a twenty-first-century subject." The film, Lee's most accessible film since *Crooklyn*, suffered at the box office, coming up against blockbusters such as *Gangs of New York* and the second part of the *Lord of the Rings* trilogy, *The Two Towers*. It earned only $13 million dollars against a $25 million dollar budget.

Sucker Free City did even worse. Intended as a pilot for a television series on Showtime, it never began production, and the film was shown at the Toronto Film Festival before being airing on television. *She Hate Me*, released in 2004, did little better, earning Lee some of the worst reviews of his career. Charles Taylor at Salon.com said that "at times, *She Hate Me* feels like the clumsiest, most amateurish movie ever made by an acclaimed director." Stephen Holden of the *New York Times* concurred, saying that "Spike Lee carries his political exasperation beyond outrage into chaos." Lee had often been criticized for trying to do and say too much in his films, and in *She Hate Me* he may have proved his critics right.

Roger Ebert, Lee's long-time defender, disagreed. He opened his review by saying that he knew that the film would get terrible reviews, but he added,

It is exciting to watch this movie. It is never boring. Lee is like a juggler who starts out with balls and gradually adds baseball bats, top hats and chainsaws. It's not an intellectual experience, but an emotional one. . . . True, the movie is not altogether successful. It's so jagged, so passionate in its ambition, it raises more questions than it answers. But isn't that better than the way most films answer more questions than they raise?

Still, with three disappointing films in a row, Lee was entering dangerous ground. To continue to receive financing for his films, he had to make movies that were financially as well as critically successful. He would come bouncing back in 2006 with two films: one a critical success and the other his biggest box-office winner to date.

10

Back on Top

The first of the two films was *Inside Man*, Lee's twentieth film in 20 years. (It is interesting to note that, although at the beginning of his career Lee denied being the "black Woody Allen," there are definite similarities. Among major directors, only Woody Allen has been as prolific a filmmaker, directing 23 feature films between 1986 and 2006. Allen is also a rabid Knicks fan and has a son named Satchel.) *Inside Man* starred three of Hollywood's biggest stars: Clive Owen, Jodie Foster, and Denzel Washington, who appeared in his fourth film for Lee. It would also be Lee's first attempt at directing a straight "genre" film.

What is a genre film? A genre film fits into a specific type of formulaic plot: westerns, science-fiction, and horror films are all examples of genre films. *Inside Man* is an example of another kind of genre—the bank robbery film, a heist that turns into a hostage crisis. Lee was brought in to direct the

Lee (right) is shown here directing Denzel Washington in *Inside Man*, a movie about a bank robbery that goes horribly wrong and turns into a hostage situation. *Inside Man* was the fourth Spike Lee movie in which Washington played a major role.

project by Brian Grazer of Imagine Entertainment, who at first questioned whether Lee, known for his individualistic style of filmmaking, was right for the job. Lee convinced Grazer that he was.

The movie opened in March 2006 to excellent reviews and great box-office success. Many reviews pointed out that, although the movie was not much more than a superior version of a genre film, Lee was still able to insert his individual style and interests into the standard formula. Kenneth Turan of the *Los Angeles Times* said:

It's obvious that Lee is more at home with argumentative, provocative, socially relevant films than he is with this kind of genre material. . . . So the director found ways to be slightly off the mark . . . [and] has been able to make political points around the film's edges, to be himself without sacrificing the project's plausibility in the process. A Sikh hostage complains of police mistreatment and being called "an Arab." Two police officers have a racially charged conversation. A boy is chided for playing a particularly brutal and insensitive video game. Not to mention that one of "Inside Man's" themes, the notion of systematic political corruption, doubtless found a receptive audience with the filmmaker.

In other words, Lee was able to take the screenplay for a standard bank robbery film, written by someone else, and still make it a "Spike Lee Joint." The film was a huge success, earning more than $88 million in the United States and nearly $200 million worldwide—Lee's biggest box-office hit to date.

Lee did not have time to enjoy his triumphant return to box-office success. He was busy putting the finishing touches on a documentary that would sum up nearly everything he had had to say as a filmmaker about the role that race plays in the United States. The film was *When the Levees Broke*, his look at the destruction caused in New Orleans by Hurricane Katrina.

THE ANGER THAT CUTS DEEPEST
It was clear to most that, if anyone in America was meant to make a documentary about Hurricane Katrina and its disastrous aftermath—caused in no small part by the government's slow response and long-term neglect—it was Spike Lee. At the time that Katrina hit, New Orleans was a mainly African-American city. African Americans were by far the group hardest hit—it was, to a large extent, an African-American tragedy.

In this still from *When the Levees Broke*, Terence Blanchard walks down a street destroyed by the hurricane, mournfully playing his trumpet.

At this stage of his career, Lee was *the* filmmaker that people turned to first when the topic was blacks in America.

After all, Lee's entire film career to date had served to shine a spotlight on the concerns of African Americans. Racism, poverty, government neglect—his films had presented these topics to a mainstream audience from the perspective of a black director for the first time in history. Hurricane Katrina and its effects on New Orleans had made clear that those problems were not problems of the past; they were still alive and active. It was up to Spike Lee to make a film that would record exactly what happened in New Orleans so that the nation and the rest of the world would never forget.

Nobody who has seen the film will ever forget. *When the Levees Broke* premiered in two parts on August 21 and 22, 2006, on HBO. It was then shown in its entirety on August 29, 2006, the one-year anniversary of Katrina's landfall. The documentary, which also screened at the Venice International Film Festival (where it won the Orizzonti Documentary Prize) and at the Toronto International Film Festival, earned Lee some of the best reviews of his career. Writing for the *Washington Post*, Lynne Duke perhaps described the film best:

> It is the anger that cuts deepest—a righteous, laser-focused anger born of betrayal, laced with sadness, a rumbling anger that pumps like blood through the veins of Spike Lee's masterly Katrina documentary, "When the Levees Broke: A Requiem in Four Acts." . . . Even when Lee's subjects are calm and composed, their words cut to the bone. It hurts to listen when Herbert Freeman Jr. describes leaving his dead mother behind at the Convention center. And most of us know her, or at least know of her, for hers was the body in the wheelchair, covered with the blanket her son had laid over her, along with the note he wrote with her name, his name and his cellphone number.
>
> Yes, it is long [four hours]. Lee has a penchant for over-long films . . . he is also a filmmaker that many love to hate or debate, a filmmaker with the kind of audacity, idiosyncrasy and racial sensibility that some find overwrought.
>
> And yet those qualities make Lee that rare director who could absorb the Katrina disaster in all its human, racial and political dimensions and make it his solemn mission to create the authoritative historical documentary. It is a lament for the dead.

IN HIS OWN WORDS...

In a 1999 interview with Bill Baxter, Lee said,

I think it is very important that films make people look at what they've forgotten.

The film, which was described by an HBO executive as one of the most important films that the company had ever made, went on to win numerous awards, including the Emmy, NAACP Image, and Peabody awards. It is, by any standards, an extraordinary achievement—and one that only Spike Lee could have accomplished.

The career of a Hollywood director is rarely long-lasting, and few ever become known to the general movie-going public. Over the course of his career, however, Lee has become an institution. He is one of only a few directors in Hollywood who can sell a film on his name alone. In addition, he has made a name for himself outside of his films: The public can easily match the name with the face. Thus, it is no wonder he has been tapped to endorse a wide variety of products.

Lee is unquestionably skilled at self-promotion, and his endorsements for products such as Levi's jeans, Ben & Jerry's ice cream, the Gap, and Nike have helped make his name and face familiar throughout the country, which in turn helps to sell his films. Unlike many other celebrities, though, he has used his business savvy and flair for publicity to help benefit the community he lives in.

Although Lee works with the Hollywood machine and the corporate mainstream, he is certainly not a part of either—as his film company, 40 Acres & a Mule Filmworks, based for a long time in predominantly black Fort Greene, proves. Lee has often criticized black celebrities (particularly Eddie Murphy) for not doing enough for African Americans within the entertainment industry. In this area, Lee has long put his money where his mouth is. Over the years, he has steadily employed black talent: cinematographer (and later director) Ernest Dickerson, costume designer Ruth E. Carter, casting director Robi Reed, scenic designer Wynn Thomas, poster designer Art Sims, production manager Preston Holmes, photographer David Lee (his brother), and writer-editor Lisa Jones, among others. He has also tried to ensure that many other black filmmakers will be turning out films in the coming years. In cowriting companion books for his films, he has tried to dispel the myth that "film is this hocus-pocus thing." He has taught courses in African-American cinema at Long Island and Harvard universities, administers a scholarship at the NYU Film School, and has awarded grants to predominantly black colleges.

Although he may sometimes moonlight as a professor and author, lend his name to a product, or take on the task of trying to "uplift the race," Lee is first and foremost a filmmaker—among his upcoming projects are a sequel to *Inside Man* and *The Miracle at St. Anna*, set in Italy in 1944, which tells the story of four black American soldiers who get trapped in an Italian village during World War II. It seems clear that Lee is planning to continue being one of the most productive and consistently interesting filmmakers in Hollywood.

Lee is also someone who knows how fortunate he is to be able to keep practicing his art. As he once said in an interview with Delroy Lindo, "Number one, I hope that I'll continue to be given the chance to make films until I don't want to make them any more. And I also say my prayers every night, that I've been fortunate to have amassed the body of work I've done, in a relatively short time." Because of him, and his pioneering efforts and the body of work that he has amassed, movies will never be the same.

Selected Filmography

STUDENT FILMS

1980   *The Answer*

1981   *Sarah*

1982   *Joe's Bed-Stuy Barbershop: We Cut Heads*

MOTION PICTURES

1986   *She's Gotta Have It*

1988   *School Daze*

1989   *Do the Right Thing*

1990   *Mo' Better Blues*

1991   *Jungle Fever*

1992   *Malcolm X*

1994   *Crooklyn*

1995   *Clockers*

1995   *Drop Squad*

1996   *The Fine Art of Separating People from Their Money*

1996   *Girl 6*

1996   *Get on the Bus*

1997   *4 Little Girls*

1998   *He Got Game*

1999   *Summer of Sam*

2000   *The Original Kings of Comedy*

2000   *Bamboozled*

2001   *The Spike Lee Collection*

2002   *Jim Brown: All American*

2002   *25th Hour*

2004   *She Hate Me*

2004   *Sucker Free City*

2006   *Inside Man*

2006   *When the Levees Broke: A Requiem in Four Acts*

MUSIC VIDEOS

1986 Branford Marsalis: "Royal Garden Blues"

1986 Miles Davis: "Tutu Medley"

1987 Anita Baker: "No One in the World"

1988 E. U.: "Da Butt"

1989 Tracy Chapman: "Born to Fight"

1989 Public Enemy: "Fight the Power"

1990 Cynda Williams: "Harlem Blues"

1991 Stevie Wonder: "Gotta Have You," "Jungle Fever," "Make Sure You're Sure"

1992 Naughty by Nature: "Hip Hop Hooray"

1994 Marc Dorsey: "People Make the World Go Round"

1994 Branford Marsalis: "Breakfast at Denny's"

1994 MCAT: "Oh My Precious"

1995 Crooklyn Dodgers: "Return of the Crooklyn Dodgers"

1995 Bruce Hornsby: "Swing Street"

1995 Chaka Khan: "Love Me Still"

COMMERCIALS

1988 Jesse Jackson political campaign

1988 Charles Barkley for Nike

1988 Michael Jordan for Nike/Air Jordan

1990–1991 Levi's 501/Buttonfly jeans series

1991 En Vogue for Diet Coke

1993 AT&T

1995 Ben & Jerry's/Smooth Ice Cream

1995 American Express/Charge Against Hunger

1995 Taco Bell/Shaquille O'Neal and Hakeem Olajuwon

2000 NFL

2002 Kmart

2003 Pepsi

1957 Lee is born Shelton Jackson Lee in Atlanta, Georgia, on March 20.

1959 The Lee family moves north and eventually settles in Brooklyn, New York.

1975 Lee graduates from John Dewey High School and enters Morehouse College, majoring in mass communications.

1977 Lee makes his first film, *Last Hustle in Brooklyn*, a 45-minute documentary.

1979 Lee graduates from Morehouse and enrolls in New York University Graduate Film School.

1980 *The Answer*, an attack on racism in the work of film pioneer D.W. Griffith creates controversy; Lee wins a teaching assistantship at NYU.

1981 Lee makes *Sarah*, a study of a Harlem family.

1982 Lee wins a student Academy Award for his third-year thesis, *Joe's Bed-Stuy Barbershop: We Cut Heads*.

1984 Lee begins his first projected full-length feature, *The Messenger*, but is forced to abandon the project after running out of money.

1985 Lee completes his first feature film, *She's Gotta Have It*.

1986 *She's Gotta Have It* opens in theaters and becomes one of the most successful independent films in history.

1988 Lee releases *School Daze*, his first studio-financed film, in association with Columbia Pictures; Lee makes his first of a series of television commercials for Nike with Michael Jordan.

1989 Lee switches to Universal Studios and releases *Do the Right Thing*.

1990 Lee releases *Mo' Better Blues*; he becomes first African American to be nominated for an Academy Award for Best Original Screenplay; he begins a campaign to direct the film biography of Malcolm X.

1991   Lee releases *Jungle Fever*.

1992   Lee releases *Malcolm X*, his most ambitious film, after a massive publicity campaign; he marries Tonya Lewis.

1994   Lee releases *Crooklyn*; his daughter Satchel is born.

1995   Lee releases *Clockers*.

1996   Lee releases *Girl 6* and *Get on the Bus*.

1997   Lee releases *4 Little Girls* and wins the Broadcast Film Critics Association Award and Golden Satellite Award for Best Documentary; his son Jackson is born.

1998   Lee receives an Academy Award nomination for Best Documentary for *4 Little Girls*; he releases *He Got Game*.

1999   Lee writes, produces, directs, and stars in *Summer of Sam*.

2000   Lee releases *The Original Kings of Comedy* and *Bamboozled*.

2002   Lee releases *25th Hour*; he publishes *Please, Baby, Please*, his first children's book with his wife.

2004   *She Hate Me* has its studio release; *Sucker Free City* is shown on television.

2006   *Inside Man* opens in theaters and becomes his biggest box-office hit to date; *When the Levees Broke: A Requiem in Four Acts* premieres on HBO

2007   Production begins on *Miracle at St. Anna*.

Aftab, Kaleem. *Spike Lee: That's My Story and I'm Sticking to It.* New York: W.W. Norton, 2006.

Bogle, Donald. *Bright Boulevards, Bold Dreams: The Story of Black Hollywood.* New York: One World/Ballantine, 2006.

———. *Toms, Coons, Bucks, Mammies, and Mulattoes: Blacks in U.S. Films.* New York: Crossroads, 1988.

Donalson, Melvin. *Black Directors in Hollywood.* Austin: University of Texas Press, 2003.

Fuchs, Cynthia. *Spike Lee Interviews.* Jackson: University Press of Mississippi, 2002.

Lee, Spike. *Best Seat in the House: A Basketball Memoir.* New York: Crown, 1997.

———. *Spike Lee's Gotta Have It.* New York: Fireside, 1987.

Lee, Spike, and Lisa Jones. *Do the Right Thing.* New York: Fireside, 1989.

———. *Mo' Better Blues.* New York: Fireside, 1990.

———. *Uplift the Race.* New York: Fireside, 1988.

Lee, Spike, and David Lee. *5 for 5.* New York: Stewart, Tabori & Chang, 1991.

Lee, Spike, and Ralph Wiley. *By Any Means Necessary.* New York: Hyperion, 1992.

Poitier, Sidney. *The Measure of a Man: A Spiritual Autobiography.* San Francisco: Harper, 2007.

X, Malcolm. *The Autobiography of Malcolm X: As Told to Alex Haley.* New York: Ballantine Books, 1987.

WEB SITES

"A Conversation With Spike Lee," NPR.org
http://www.npr.org/templates/story/story.php?storyId=5317036

"When the Levees Broke: Interview with Spike Lee," HBO.com
www.hbo.com/docs/programs/whentheleveesbroke/interview.html

PAGE

A

Academy Awards
  Do the Right Thing, 52–53
  4 Little Girls, 101
  Singleton nomination, 72
  student, 20
advertisements, 4, 37, 42–43, 101, 116
African Americans
  as actors, 32–33, 47, 48–49, 54, 60–61
  control of black-themed films by, 76–78
  divisions within community, 99
  as filmmakers, 15, 16, 25–27, 45–46, 71–73, 116–117
  Hurricane Katrina and, 2–4, 113–114
  issues with *Malcolm X,* 79–81
  jazz and, 56
  Lee as spokesperson, 3–4, 50–51
  Million Man March, 98
  as portrayed by Hollywood, 18–19, 24, 54, 56–57, 60–61, 79
  skin color issues, 31–32, 39–42, 68
  on television, 43
  women as portrayed by Lee, 33–35, 43, 62, 98
  See also racism
Allen, Woody, 31, 111
Anarchy in the Bronx. See Summer of Sam (film)
Ansen, David, 51
The Answer (film), 18–19, 106–107
anti-Semitism, 62–63
Araton, Harvey, 102–103
Armey, Dick, 7
The Autobiography of Malcolm X (Haley), 14

B

Bamboozled (film), 72, 106–109
bank robbery films, 111–113
Baraka, Amiri, 79–80

basketball, 101–103
Bassinger, Kim, 52–53
Belafonte, Harry, 60
Bensonhurst incident, 65–67, 70
The Best Seat in the House: A Basketball Memoir (Lee), 103
Birmingham church bombing, 100
The Birth of a Nation (film), 18–19, 106–107
Black College: The Talented Tenth (film), 16
black face, 107
blaxploitation films, 27, 72
Bogle, Donald, 24, 63
Boy Scouts, 12–13
Boyz n the Hood (film), 72

C

Canby, Vincent, 86
Cannes Film Festival, 30–31
Carmen Jones (film), 32–33
Carroll, Kathleen, 68
Chicago Film Critics Association, 86–87
Clark, Mike, 86
Clockers (film), 95–97
Colored Literary and Industrial School, 9
Columbia Pictures, 38, 42–44
Completion Bond Company (CBC), 82
Crooklyn (film), 6, 89, 90–95

D

Dandridge, Dorothy, 32–33
Davis, Ossie
  in films by Lee, 47, 48, 85
  on Lee, 6
Dee, Ruby, 47, 48
Dickerson, Ernest
  commercial films, 49, 59, 62
  student films, 19–20
Dinkins, David, 52, 67
Do the Right Thing (film)
  Academy Awards and, 52–53

breakthrough nature of, 5–6
inspiration for, 46
plot and characters, 47–49
reviews, 51–52
documentaries by Lee, 3–4, 16–17,
113–116
drug issues, 69
Duke, Lynne, 115

E

Ebert, Roger
on *Bamboozled,* 108
on *Crooklyn,* 95
on *Do the Right Thing,* 51
on *Get on the Bus,* 99
on *Girl 6,* 97–98
on *He Got Game,* 103
on *Jungle Fever,* 70
on Lee, 85
on *Malcolm X,* 83, 85–86
on *She Hate Me,* 109–110
on *Summer of Sam,* 105
education, 9, 13–15, 16–20
Edwards, William James "Willie"
(great-grandfather), 9
Eichelberger, Herb, 16

F

Farrakhan, Louis, 98
Field, Sally, 51
film festivals. See *specific festivals*
films, Hollywood
African American filmmakers,
15, 16, 25–27, 45–46, 71–73,
116–117
costs, 22–23
Malcolm X proposal, 74–76
portrayal of African Americans,
18–19, 24, 54, 56–57, 60–61,
79
films by Lee
African-American life in, 29
African Americans employed in
making, 116
as biography of Lee, 8
breakthrough nature of, 5–6

documentaries, 3–4, 16–17,
113–116
financing, 20, 23, 37–38
motivation for, 19
signature shot, 61–62
for television, 6, 99–101, 113–
116
while at Morehouse College, 15,
16–17
while at NYU, 18–20
See also *specific films*
Folkes, George, 15
40 Acres & A Mule Filmworks, 34,
35, 116
4 Little Girls (film), 6, 100–101
Fuller, Charles, 76

G

Gates, Henry Louis, Jr., 72
genre films, 111
George, Nelson, 29, 32–33
Get on the Bus (film), 98–99
Girl 6 (film), 97–98
Graff, Keir, 6–7
Griffith, Michael, 46
Guess Who's Coming to Dinner
(film), 60–61
Gumbel, Bryant, 43

H

Haley, Alex, 14
Harris, Erich Leon, 61
Hawkins, Yusef, 65–66, 70
HBO, 101, 114–116
He Got Game (film), 103–104
Hernández, Juano, 56, 60
Holden, Stephen, 108–109
Homecoming (screenplay). See
School Daze (film)
Howard Beach incident, 46
Hurricane Katrina, 1–4, 6, 113–
116

I

"I Am Not an Anti-Semite" (Spike
Lee), 63

Image award, 116
Inside Man (film), 111–113
Island Pictures
   School Daze and, 37–38
   She's Gotta Have It and, 30, 31, 37
It's Homecoming (screenplay). See *School Daze* (film)

J

Jewison, Norman, 76–78
Jews, 31, 62–63
Joe's Bed-Stuy Barbershop: We Cut Heads (film), 20
John Dewey High School, 14–15
Johns, Tracy Camilla, 31–32
Jordan, Michael, 4, 37
Jungle Fever (film)
   breakthrough nature of, 5
   plot and characters, 67–70
   success, 70–71

K

Kaplan, Susan (stepmother), 92
King, Martin Luther, Jr., 50
Klein, Joe, 51–52
Knicks, 101–103
Koch, Ed, 67

L

LaSalle, Mick, 109
Last Hustle in Brooklyn (documentary), 16–17
The Learning Tree (film), 26–27
Lee, Arnold (brother), 11
Lee, Bill (father)
   as jazz musician, 9–11
   music for son's films, 41, 59–60
   racism and, 12
   relationship with, 13, 36–37, 92
   on Spike's size, 13
Lee, Chris (brother), 11
Lee, Cinque (brother), 11, 37, 91–92
Lee, David (brother), 11

Lee, Jackson (son), 101
Lee, Jacquelyn Shelton (mother), 9–11, 12, 13, 15–16
Lee, Joie (sister), 11
   as actor, 36, 58, 61
   Crooklyn and, 91–92
Lee, Satchel (daughter), 89
Lee, Shelton Jackson "Spike"
   accusations against, 6
   ancestors, 8–9
   awards, 20, 30–31, 52, 86–87, 115, 116
   birth, 9
   childhood, 11–13
   marriage, 89
   nickname, 11
   personality, 11–12, 13, 31, 37, 89–90
Lee, Tonya Lewis (wife), 6, 89
Lee (grandmother), 12
Long Island incident, 70
Los Angeles Critics awards, 52
Lott, Trent, 6

M

Malcolm X
   importance to Lee, 14
   overview of life, 77
   on violence and self-defense, 50
Malcolm X (film)
   breakthrough nature of, 6, 78–79
   controversy about, 79–80, 82–83
   as epic, 83–85
   financing, 81–82
   initial proposal, 74–77
   Lee on, 87
   reviews, 83, 85–86
   success, 86–87, 88
The Maroon Tiger (Morehouse College newspaper), 14
Marsalis, Branford, 13
Maslin, Janet, 43
message films, 26–27
The Messenger (film), 22–23

Micheaux, Oscar, 24–25
Mike (ancestor), 8–9
Miller, Reggie, 101–102
Million Man March, 98
minstrel shows, 107
Mo' Better Blues (film), 58–59, 62, 63–64
Morehouse College, 14–15, 16–17, 38
music
  father and, 9–11, 13
  for *He Got Game*, 104
  jazz films, 55, 56
  lessons during childhood of Lee, 11
  in *School Daze*, 40, 41
  videos, 101
  See also *Mo' Better Blues*

N
Nagin, Ray, 2
National Association for the Advancement of Colored People (NAACP), 18, 116
Nevins, Sheila, 4
New Jack Cinema, 72–72
New Orleans, Louisiana, 1–4, 113–115
New York Film Critics circle, 87
New York University (NYU) Graduate Film School, 16–20
Nothing But a Man (film), 26–27

O
O'Hehir, Andrew, 108
The Original Kings of Comedy (film), 106
Orizzonti Documentary Prize, 115

P
Peabody award, 116
Phoebe (ancestor), 9
Picker, David, 38
Please, Baby, Please (Lee and Lee), 6

Please, Puppy, Please (Lee and Lee), 6
Poitier, Sidney, 27, 60–61
Pollard, Sam, 96, 97
Price, Richard, 95, 96
Prix de Jeunesse for Best New Film, 30–31
Puttnam, David, 42

R
race movies, 25–26
racism
  Bensonhurst incident, 65–67, 70
  Birmingham church bombing, 100
  in *The Birth of a Nation*, 18–19
  within black community, 31–32, 39–42, 68
  experienced by Lee, 12–13
  in Hollywood system, 20, 40, 52–53
  Howard Beach incident, 46
  Lee accused of, 62–63
  Long Island incident, 70
  Malcolm X and, 77, 78, 85
  public debate, 88
  as theme of films by Lee, 49–50, 67–68, 99, 106–107
  See also portrayal of African Americans under films, Hollywood
Robeson, Paul, 25–26, 60
Ross, Monty, 14–15, 37–38

S
San Francisco International Film Festival, 30
Sarah (film), 19–20
School Daze (film)
  basis, 15
  breakthrough nature of, 5
  filming, 38
  financing, 37–38
  music, 40, 41
  plot and characters, 38–39, 40

promoting, 42–43
reviews, 43
success, 43–44, 45
Schultz, Michael, 27
Scorsese, Martin, 16, 95
Screen Actors Guild, 22–23
Sharpton, Al, 66–67
She Hate Me (film), 109–110
Shelton, Zimmie (grandmother), 15
She's Gotta Have It (film)
breakthrough nature of, 5, 24
children's book based on, 6
financing, 28–29
plot and characters, 27–28
reviews, 31–34
success, 30–31, 34–36
Siegel, Joel, 95
Sinclair, Abiola, 33
Singleton, John, 72
Siskel, Gene, 95
Smith, Earl, 14–15
Snow Hill, Alabama, 12
Snow Hill Institute, 9
Spike DDB, 101
Spike's Joint/Spike's Joint West, 29
Steel, Dawn, 42
"Straight and Nappy" (Bill Lee), 41
Sucker Free City (film), 109
Summer of Sam (film), 6, 104–105

T
Taylor, Charles, 109
television movies, 6, 99–101, 113–116
themes of films by Lee, 5–6
class conflict, 40, 41, 70

family life, 6, 92–93
racism, 49–50, 67–68, 99, 106–107
scapegoating, 104–105
sexuality, 60, 61, 67, 70
Time (magazine), 14
Toms, Coons, Bucks, Mammies, and Mulattoes (Bogle), 24
Toronto International Film Festival, 115
Turan, Kenneth, 112–113
25th Hour (film), 109

U
United Front to Preserve the Legacy of Malcolm X, 79–80
Universal Pictures, 55

V
Venice International Film Festival, 115
violence, 49–50, 72

W
Warner Brothers Pictures, 74, 78, 81, 82–83
Washington, Booker T., 9
Washington, Denzel
Academy Award and, 54
in Lee's films, 58, 61, 103, 111
as Malcolm X, 76, 79, 87
When the Levees Broke: A Requiem in Four Acts (documentary television film), 3–4, 113–116
Wilson, August, 77–78
Wilson, Woodrow, 18
Worth, Marvie, 60, 74

About the Author

Dennis Abrams is the author of several books for Chelsea House, including biographies of Barbara Park, Anthony Horowitz, Hamid Karzai, and the Beastie Boys. He attended Antioch College, where he majored in English and communications. A voracious reader since the age of three, Abrams lives in Houston, Texas, with his partner of 19 years, along with their two dogs and three cats.